January 2016

Nanette

I'm so glad to share

THE JOURNEY

Growing Up in Christ

(not an iron witty
wondrous leaders!

Deborah Anne Rundlett

with love,

Debbie

Produced in partnership with the Perichoresis Network
and Muskingum Valley Presbytery
Voice: 330.339.5515 | Email: Deborah@MVPJourney.org
Web: www.MVPJourney.org and www.DeborahRundlett.com

ISBN: 1495222829
ISBN-13: 978-1495222825

DEDICATION

The Journey: Growing Up in Christ is dedicated with love and thanks to all with whom I have shared the journey in Christ. Specific thanks go to my family – Dick and Elizabeth – and Muskingum Valley Presbytery and the wonderful team with whom I serve – Paula, Candice and Barb. Pilgrim blessings!

.

CONTENTS

Appendices

DEBORAH ANNE RUNDLETT

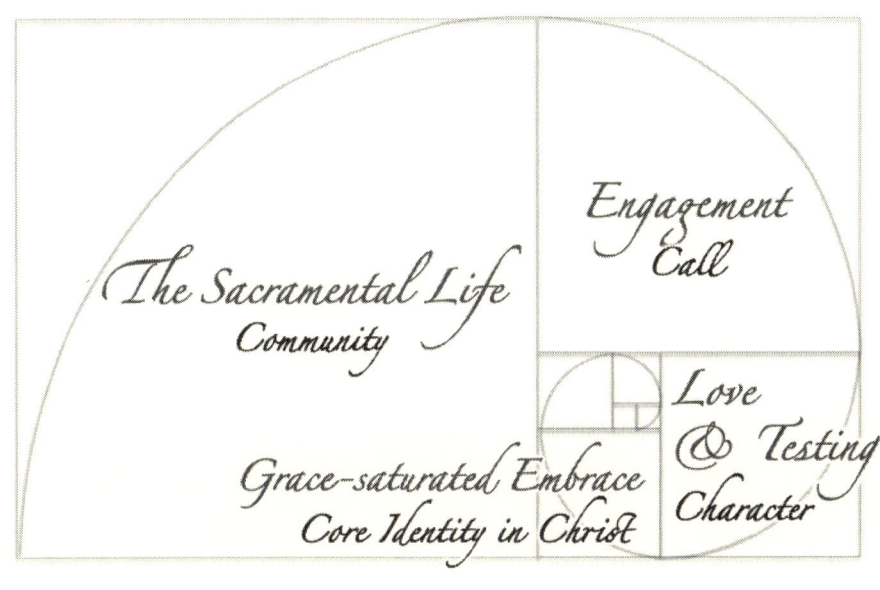

The Sacramental Life

Community

Engagement
Call

Love
& Testing
Character

Grace-saturated Embrace
Core Identity in Christ

WITH GRATITUDE

Gratitude is the heart's memory.
French Proverb

The concept for the formational journey came from the work of Dr. Terry Wardle, Professor of Practical Theology and Director of the Institute of Formational Counseling at Ashland Theology Seminary. So simple and yet so profound, Jesus' earthly journey models for us the means by which we are to grow up in Christ. Through the formational journey, Terry both invites and challenges disciple-making leaders to become like Jesus.

I had the joy and privilege of teaching in the Masters of Divinity cohort with Terry. His greatest passion is to nurture a spiritual maturity in his students that will see them through the challenges of ministry. With over 18,000 pastors leaving the ministry each year, this is no small challenge.

For several years, I pressed Terry to write a book about the formational journey of Jesus. His response was that it was not his book to write. In the meantime, I began to incorporate the concept of the formational journey of Jesus into not only my teaching, but also my coaching and equipping of pastor-leader teams. This collection of reflections is born out of that work.

It has been said that gratitude is the heart's memory. I am grateful to Terry— not only for inviting me deeper into my own formational journey, but also for the challenge to develop this material as an invitation to others. To my colleague and friend, thank you! You have blessed me more than you can imagine. You and Cheryl both reside in my heart's memory!

These materials were first developed in conjunction with a leadership retreat for Christ Presbyterian Church in Canton, Ohio. This downtown congregation intuitively understood that core identity in Christ must come before all else. I am deeply thankful for the opportunity to serve as a theologian-in-residence and for the journey shared over the last eight years.

Additional thanks must be given to two presbyteries dear to my heart: Muskingum Valley Presbytery and Peace River Presbytery. These two presbyteries have blessed me by their willingness to journey through these materials, providing feedback and insight into their development. In particular, I give thanks for Dave deVries, Graham Hart, Anita Howard, Paula Lane, Candice McMath and Barb Schie—gifted colleagues whose insights have been invaluable. And, of course, thanks to my family who supported me through the writing of *The Journey*!

With love in Christ,

Deborah Anne Rundlett
Advent 2013
New Philadelphia, Ohio

INTRODUCTION

From Dr. Terry Wardle

It has been nearly four decades since I "accepted Christ," a term used often back then to identify one's conversion to Christianity. I was a young man finishing college and had been drawn to faith by the lives of several believing friends. The difference between their values and mine was obvious, as was their sense of peace and purpose, which contrasted with my deep inner turmoil and confusion. Late one snowy winter night, after wrestling with "the decision," I walked across campus to an apartment where my friends lived and surrendered my life to Christ. I sensed the presence of the Lord and knew that something had awakened within me: a quickening of the Spirit that was real, and yet (in many ways) indescribable.

That night, I became a "true believer," even though I was far from certain what that actually meant. My friends were genuinely excited and committed to disciple me (another concept that was somewhat vague but seemed critically important). The foundation of this discipleship rested on two dominant concepts. First, there was a whole lot of information I needed to know—about God, Jesus, sin, holiness, and countless other matters of faith. (If there been some divine exam on the essentials of Christian belief, I would certainly have failed! I needed to study Christian history and theology to become a good and faithful disciple.)

Second, my friends were insistent that there were a number of things I now needed to do. They gave me a little book that spelled these out, including activities like going to church, reading my bible, tithing, witnessing, and (of course) praying. "Real Christians do these things." If I was to be a *real Christian*, I would need to do these things. My friends committed to helping me along the way. They were kind, yet they made it clear that I needed to change. I agreed. I knew better than they that my life was a contradiction to Christian faith, so change was obviously needed. And the foundation of this change seemed to rest on my willingness to learn more and do more, as each related to being a Christian.

I am deeply grateful that I had friends that cared enough to invest in me. And it certainly was important that I grasped the fundamentals of faith and embraced lifestyle changes like those prescribed. But over the years I have discovered that increasing one's knowledge of Christian belief, and even performing various Christian activities like going to church, praying, and witnessing are simply not enough. They are important, yes, but knowledge and activities are inadequate. And here is why:

Changing one's level of knowledge and behaviors can be accomplished by human effort: If you strive enough, perform enough, study enough, and do enough, things can and will change. But what I need (and, for that matter, what every person needs) at the very deepest level of life is not change, but *transformation.*

Transformation does not happen because we have learned truths and embraced Christian behavior. Transformation involves ongoing encounters with God, where He does in us what we can never do in ourselves. Learning theological concepts can increase our knowledge and shape our beliefs. Engaging in Christian activities is important, but by themselves, they simply change our behavior. But when people encounter the presence of God in the episodes of life, transformation takes place. It is not our knowledge or behavior that is different: *We* are different—at the level of identity, character, virtues, values, and ultimately vocation.

The Christian life is best described as a developmental journey, in which we surrender to the daily transforming touch of Christ and increasingly grow up in Him. Every day, in countless ways, the Lord positions us for transformation, using "all things" of life to accomplish His purpose. Our developmental journey (or as I call it, "formational journey,") begins even before we have made a decision to follow Christ, as the Spirit begins to woo us into the loving embrace of the Father. This journey continues until the day we see Him face to face, all the while forming the surrendered person into the likeness of Christ.

The formational journey is best understood by likening it to human development. On this pilgrimage of faith we move through different stages, easily identified as infancy, childhood, adolescence, young adulthood, and ultimately adulthood. Each stage presents the follower of Christ with opportunities to surrender to needed levels of transformation, each stage building upon the next. Cooperating with the Lord in the developmental growth of one stage best positions the believer to move forward to deeper transformation and Christian growth in the next stage.

Years ago, as I began to consider the Christian life as a formational journey of transformation, the Holy Spirit drew my attention to the life of Christ himself. It should have been obvious that if we are to grow up in Christ, some attention should be given to the doorways of growth our Lord experienced as he lived his life. Scripture soon gave up its treasure, presenting numerous passages in the life of Christ that would be essential for the development of any mature Christ follower. It was this combination—a developmental view of Christian growth and the model of Christ's life—that gave birth to the essential elements of what is now known as the formational journey.

As I taught the formational journey over recent years, many people found it a helpful contribution to Christian formation. But frankly, no one was more enthusiastic or insistent that there be more done with the concept than Dr. Deborah Rundlett. If Debbie was in the crowd when I shared this idea, immediately (and repeatedly!) she wanted to know when I would be writing a book about the formational journey. And my answer was always the same: "Debbie, you should do it."

Dr. Deborah Rundlett is first and foremost a cherished friend and colleague. I have enjoyed numerous professional and personal interactions with her and have always come away the richer. I have been deeply impressed by her devotion to Christ, her vibrant spirit, her keen mind, and her dedication to the church. Frankly, she is one of a kind. When Debbie told me that she was saying yes to writing this book, I could not have been more thrilled. Because of all she brings to the task, this book was always hers to write.

The Journey: Growing Up in Christ is a wonderful contribution to the family of Christ. It sets forth the transformational nature of Christian formation, building upon the life of Christ and helping believers say yes to being spiritually formed as followers of Jesus. This marvelous resource is biblically grounded, theologically faithful, and, most importantly, alive with the Spirit. It is a resource that will help Christians move from belief and behavior change to deep levels of identity and character formation. I wholeheartedly recommend this resource to believers walking the journey toward Christ and his likeness.

Dr. Deborah Rundlett will find, that because of this fine work, generations of Christians to come will rise up and call her blessed. And, with that said, let me be the first. Debbie, you, my friend, are a special gift!

Terry Wardle
Ashland, Ohio
January 2014

PREFACE

It has been said that the gospel, in summary, is to become like Jesus. So simple, and yet so difficult! How on earth are we to become like Jesus?

The Journey: Growing Up in Christ looks at the earthly journey of Jesus as a model for how we are to grow up in Christ. We begin with *An Invitation,* to prepare us to heed Jesus' call to follow him, and follow by tracking his earthly journey that it might inform our faith journey. *The Journey* is divided into six sections:

- *An Invitation*
- *The Grace-Saturated Embrace*
- *Love & Testing*
- *Engagement*
- *The Sacramental Life*
- *Resurrection Blessings*

All too often, we focus on developing "competencies" for mission and ministry ahead of nurturing core identity in Christ. In a time when 18,000 pastors leave the ministry each year and untold others leave the church, it behooves us to begin with who and whose we are in Christ. Only then can our characters be transformed, our calls discerned, and our competencies developed.

Within each one of us there is a yearning to make a difference. Heeding God's call begins by following Jesus. While gifting and passions are important, God's call is first and foremost an invitation to enter into the divine embrace that we might never doubt that each and every one of us is "of the Father's love begotten!"

The Journey: Growing Up in Christ is an open conversation. I would love to hear from you about your journey. In what way have these materials been helpful to you in your faith journey? Are there materials you would like to share? If so, please email me at Deborah@MVPJourney.org. I look forward to hearing from you!

Blessings on the journey!
Deborah Anne Rundlett

The Journey:
Growing Up in Christ

An Invitation

Engagement
Call

The Sacramental Life
Community

Love
& Testing
Character

Grace-saturated Embrace
Core Identity in Christ

DEBORAH ANNE RUNDLETT

TWO METAPHORS

God made humanity because God loves stories.
Hebrew Midrash, as told by Elie Wiesel

When our daughter Elizabeth was little, she would daily press her father and me to tell her a story. Not just any story, but her story. This request often came at bedtime, but it also came at the dinner table or while on long drives. To this day, telling stories is one of our favorite family activities.

We tell of how we long awaited and anticipated her birth. We share in detail the day she was born (nine days late on my birthday) when Drs. Jose and Maria, father and daughter, fought over who got to deliver her. (The father won!) We describe the snowstorm that blanketed New York and Connecticut on the weekend of her baptism. We report how people came from near and far, in spite of the snow, to celebrate her birth and participate in her baptism. We talk about God's call to make the journey our home, a journey that has taken us from Connecticut to New York, Pittsburgh, San Diego, and now Ohio.

Not only does Elizabeth love to hear the stories of her life, but those of her parents, her grandparents, her aunts and uncles and cousins. For in those stories, she knows that she belongs. She knows that she is loved and a part of something greater than herself

But as precious as those stories are, they cannot be fully understood apart from knowing the story of God's love for her and for all creation. As John the Baptist reminds us: "This is how much God loved the world: He gave his Son, his one and only Son. And this is why: so that no one need be destroyed; by believing in him, anyone can have a whole and lasting life" (John 3:16, The Message).

This is the story that informs her—and our—story. It is the story that gives her life meaning and purpose and direction. This is the story that helps her make sense of life's complexity and challenge. By this story, she knows that her core identity rests in Christ alone. She knows that as she walks in his path, her character will reflect the fruit of the Spirit.

As psychologist Daniel Siegel notes, the "sharing of stories reflects the central importance of narratives in creating coherence in human life and connecting our minds to each other. Stories are passed from one generation to another and help keep the human soul alive" (The Developing Mind). We are a storied people. As the old Hebrew Midrash tells us: God made us because God loves stories.

What are the stories that have shaped you and made you who you are today? What narrative cycles in scripture best inform your understanding of who and whose you are in Christ? How will these narratives guide your journey?

Food for the Journey
- John 1:1-21, The prologue of John

Journey Preparations: Know Your Story
"Now, with God's help, I shall become myself" (Søren Kierkegaard).

There is an old saying: "You are what you eat." The same is true of memory: We are what we remember. The stories of our life and faith provide the bridge between who we are and who God is calling us to become. If we are to grow up into maturity in Christ, we need to know our story—born out of the intersection of our life's journey and God's Word to us.

As you prepare to journey with Jesus, take time to remember who and whose you are. Set aside some time to gather with those you love and share the stories that make you who you are. And then share THE Story! Read through the narratives of Jesus' birth found in Luke 1-2 and Matthew 1-2, and give thanks!

Prayer for the Journey
Inhabit my heart, O God, as you inhabited human flesh.
Be here among us with all of your wisdom, all of your power,
all of your mercy, all of your love,
that we might learn to be like you from Jesus who came to be like us.
Holy are you. Holy are we who are called to become like Jesus. Amen.
Miriam Therese Winter (adapted)

JOURNEY PREPARATIONS

Prepare the way for the Lord, make straight paths for him.
Mark 1:3

Checklist
- ☐ Destination: Christ Formed in Us
- ☐ Itinerary: The Formational Journey
- ☐ Terrain: The Importance of Conditioning
- ☐ Compass: The 4C's
- ☐ Packing Instructions: Be a Pilgrim, Not a Tourist.

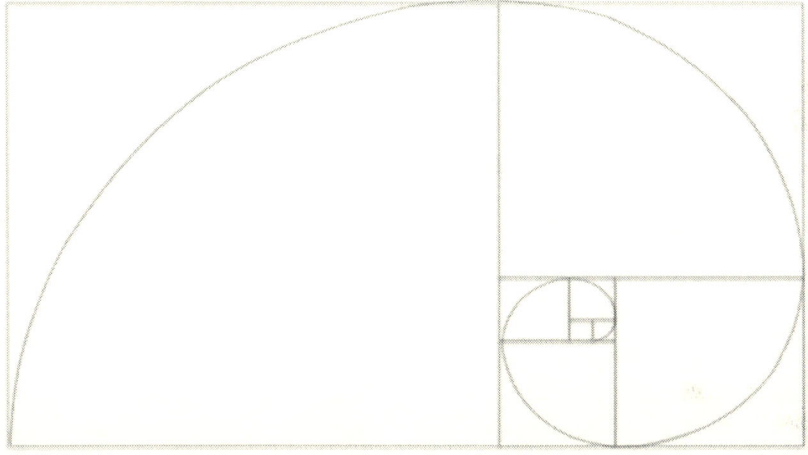

DESTINATION: CHRIST FORMED IN US

I labor until Christ is formed in you.
Galatians 4:19

I have always loved to travel. Be it a day trip or transatlantic, by foot or by car, by train or by plane, even the anticipation of travel fills me with excitement. Throughout our marriage, Dick and I have called the journey our home. It is a journey that has taken us across the country from East coast to West coast and through the Midwest. Still, the most significant journey has been the one we have shared in Christ.

The Journey. Each of us must make of it what we will. Each of us must choose the path by which we will travel. Our paths meander inward and outward, upward and forward. The longest journey we take, however, is the journey inward to a destination is not a place but rather a state of being, in which Christ is formed in us and we in Christ. Will we allow this formation to take place, or not? Poet Mary Oliver presses: "Tell me, what is it you plan to do with your one wild and precious life?"

The Greek word for "form" refers to the inward and real formation of the essential nature of a person. We cannot become our real selves—the people we are created to be by God—apart from Christ. The Apostle Paul uses the word form in a number of places, including Galatians, where he writes: "I labor until Christ is formed in you" (4:19). I labor, the apostle exhorts, until your core identity is formed in Christ, your character transformed, your call discerned, and your competencies (your God-given strengths and gifts) developed. What is it you plan to do with your one wild and precious life?

Henri Nouwen has said that the gospel, simply stated, is to become like Jesus: Will you become like Jesus? It is as simple and difficult as that! You have only to follow the path provided by God in Christ. "In the fullness of time, God sent the Son" that we might know the way (Galatians 4:4). Through his incarnation is our formation. Through his earthly journey, he invites us to follow him that we might be "transformed into his likeness with ever-increasing glory" (II Corinthians 3:18).

"Come, follow me!" Jesus calls us. The journey is nigh!

Journey preparations

Pause and ponder Paul's words to the Galatians: "I labor until Christ is formed in you." Who labors that Christ might be formed in you? For whom, do you labor? In what ways do you reflect the formation of Christ in your life? What is it you plan to do with your one wild and precious life?

Prayer for the Journey

God, help me to change.
To know the need for it.
To deal with the pain of it.
To experience the joy of it.
To undertake the journey without knowing the destination.
The art of gentle revolution.
Michael Leunig, <u>A Common Prayer</u>

ITINERARY: THE FORMATIONAL JOURNEY

i-tin-er-ar-y /ī'tinə,rerē/ *noun*
1. A planned route or journey.
2. A travel document recording these.

Sculptor Henry Moore once said that "the secret of life is to have a task, something you devote your whole life to, something you bring everything to, every minute of the day for your whole life. And the most important thing is that it must be something you cannot possibly do." Such is the nature of our life journey to become like Jesus: it is seemingly impossible, yet this is God's call to us. It is a calling that demands every minute, every breath. And so, the journey beckons.

By nature, I am a planner and a list maker. Not that I dislike spontaneity, it's just that I cannot help but organize. The wisdom Louis Pasteur applied to science also applies to pilgrimage. He found that "In the field of observation, chance favors the prepared mind." Thus, while every trip begins with dreaming and has its unexpected moments, it is essential to plan. The gift of Jesus' earthly life is that it provides us with an itinerary for our formational journey in Christ, complete with markers along the way:

From Bethlehem to Egypt to Nazareth; to Jerusalem, the River Jordan and the Wilderness; to the Sea of Galilee, the towns and villages, the lonely places and stormy seas. On to Bethany, Bethsaida and Samaria to Mount Tabor, the Upper Room, Gethsemane, and Golgotha. Then to a tomb found empty, through closed doors, and breakfast on the beach. Jesus shows us the way. We know the story; it is our story. But have we made the journey?

Just as Jesus was born, so also we must be born in the Spirit. Just as community gathered to celebrate and consecrate his birth, so the call of God is to be in community that together we might celebrate and consecrate—something we must first experience if we are to share this gift with others. Likewise, the community is called to protect against threats and provide opportunities for growth. Only then will we be ready to heed God's call as Jesus did in his baptism, where in the intersection of gifts with the needs of others the Father's love will be made known.

Welsh hymn writer, Brian Wren, believes that to embark on the formational journey, we must begin with the end in mind: "Sing my song backwards, from end to beginning, Friday to Monday, from dying to birth." To live resurrection requires that we journey through death. It is not an itinerary for the faint of heart. Still, if we are to become like Jesus, it is the only way.

For some, the journey will follow a progression from one stage of formation to the next. For others, it will require a more circuitous route. Even so, we must be willing to be flexible, sometimes lingering in a place, other times moving on ahead, only later to return that we might know that place for the first time. If necessary, we need to be willing to lose our way that we might be found. Whatever the route, to undertake the journey is to open ourselves to the movement of the Spirit in our midst. It is to find ourselves changed—transformed—until, degree by degree, we become like Jesus.

Journey preparations

1. Do you have an itinerary for your life's journey?
2. How might the itinerary of Jesus' earthly journey inform your journey?
3. Using the map below, reflect on your journey to date. In what ways has your journey mirrored Jesus' earthly journey? In what ways has it differed? Are there gaps? Are there places you need to return to for nurture, healing, even reconciliation?

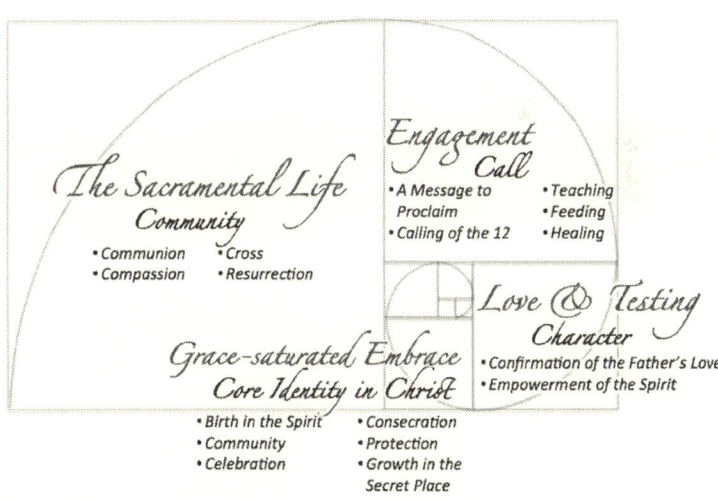

Prayer for the Journey

Take, O take me as I am.
Summon out what I shall be.
Set your seal upon my heart.
And live in me.
John Bell, Iona; Song of Songs

17

TERRAIN: THE IMPORTANCE OF CONDITIONING

Search me, God, and know my heart;
test me and know my anxious thoughts.
See if there is any offensive way in me
and lead me in the way everlasting.
Psalm 139:23-24

As those who have journeyed on ahead know, the terrain is not always smooth. Scripture describes in detail the conditions of our route. The trip from Nazareth to Jerusalem alone is 64 miles "as the crow flies," but over 90 miles when taken by foot. When south of Nazareth, one goes "up to Jerusalem" (Matthew 20:17-19) as the city rests on a mountainous terrain at high elevation (over 2,000 feet above sea level). From crowded cities to quiet waters, desolate places through stormy seas, God leads us. We do well to prepare physically, emotionally, mentally and spiritually for this journey, for the journey will test us, body, mind, and soul.

As we come to learn, the journey's terrain provides a landscape that brings us face to face with who we are. To steal an image born of a movie title, we are confronted with "the good, the bad, and the ugly" within ourselves. As Jan Richardson writes: The journey "doesn't allow for leaving our internal landscape behind; instead, it confronts us with whatever distortions and brokenness we have allowed to creep into our terrain" (2010). If we were not previously committed to conditioning of body, mind and soul before, we quickly come to understand both the need and the importance of a daily rhythm.

Jim Loehr and Tony Schwartz in The Power of Full Engagement believe that body, mind and soul are interconnected, and that we need to be stewards of our energy in this life's journey. They write, "To be fully engaged, we must be physically energized, emotional connected, mentally focused, and spiritually aligned with a purpose beyond our immediate self-interest[. ... This] requires strength, endurance, flexibility, and resilience in all dimensions" (2003, Loc. 195; p. 288).

Serious athletes engage in a regime of cross training, often working out with both weights and through cardio exercises to build muscle and endurance. But that is not all. They must also attend to mental and emotional stamina; for this, mindfulness is needed. So also, those preparing to journey with

Jesus need to commit to a regimen of cross-training, beginning with daily immersion into the Word, unceasing prayer, service to community, as well as care of body, mind and soul. As we will learn, the journey's terrain will confront us with the need to develop holy habits and rhythms by which to both stretch and sustain ourselves as we seek to become like Jesus.

Contrary to popular thought, "stress is not the enemy in our lives[. ... Rather,] it is the key to growth. In order to build strength in a muscle we must systematically stress it, expending energy beyond normal levels. To build capacity, we must allow for both stress and recovery—so long as it is followed by adequate recovery" (Loehr & Schwartz). First, we push beyond our normal limits, followed by time for renewal. How will you build capacity for your journey with Jesus? What habits will help you to nurture a deeper relationship with God in Christ? How will you balance your need for both stress and renewal in your formational journey?

Journey Preparations

William Paulsell notes, "It is unlikely that we will deepen our relationship with God in a casual or haphazard manner. There will be a need for some intentional commitment and some reorganization in our own life" (1987). If we are to seriously commit to this journey, we must be intentional about our conditioning. Just as athletes develop training regimens, so a "rule of life" provides us with a way to partner with God that Christ might be formed in us. In a very real sense, our practices become our path.

This next week, take some time to look at the rhythm of Jesus' earthly life. What holy habits or disciplines does he reflect in his daily rhythm? How did they shape what he did or didn't do? How did his "rule of life" condition him for the times of stress and challenge on his earthly journey? How did they prepare him to follow in the way of the cross? How might Jesus' spiritual "conditioning" inform our "conditioning" as we prepare for The Journey?

Prayer for the Journey

Dear God, we pray for another way of being; another way of knowing.
Across the difficult terrain of our existence
we have attempted to build a highway
and in doing so have lost our footpath.
God, lead us to our foot path: lead us where in simplicity
we may move at the speed of natural creatures
and feel the earth's love beneath our feet.

Lead us where, step-by-step,
we may feel the movement of creation in our hearts.
And lead us where, side-by-side, we may feel
the embrace of the common soul.
Nothing can be loved at speed.
God lead us to the slow path; to the joyous insights of the pilgrims;
another way of knowing; another way of being.
Amen.
Michael Leunig

COMPASS: THE 4C'S

Fixing our eyes on Jesus, the pioneer and perfecter of our faith.
Hebrews 12:2

"Fixing our eyes on Jesus"—It is as simple as that. The problem is that we can't always "see" him; though present, he is beyond our horizon. Other times, just as a breeze can take a boat off course, life ever so slightly shifts our attention off Jesus and takes us off our intended destination. Still other times, there are strong winds or other conditions that blow our lives off course. Whether we lose our way through our own actions or external circumstances, a compass can help us recalibrate our lives back towards Jesus.

Those who have journeyed on ahead can attest to the reality that a map or GPS is of limited help when seeking to follow Jesus. The journey is not about getting from point A to point B in the shortest amount of time. It is about becoming like Jesus; being transformed, degree by degree, until we reflect the image of Christ (II Corinthians 3:17-18).

Ultimately, becoming like Jesus is not something we can do in our own strength or on our own schedule. It can only be accomplished in and through the power of the Holy Spirit. To be sure, our full participation is required. But such participation calls for a willingness to follow the course set before us. This is why a compass calibrated to "core identity in Christ" is helpful in navigating the journey. Core identity in Christ, along with character transformation, call, and competence provide the four cardinal points that direct our path home to God as we live the questions of the fourfold journey[1]:

- Core Identity: Who am I?
- Character Transformation: With whom are my core relationships?
- Call: What are my strengths?
- Competence: What is my legacy?

These questions are answered as Christ is formed in us. Scripture is our compass, the means by which we come to know our story in his story. Not doctrine, not tradition, not culture, but *scripture*. God in Christ is our True North in the midst of a chaotic and unpredictable world. As the poet queries: "Where is the wisdom we have lost in knowledge?" (T.S. Eliot).

---

[1] "The Four C's" concept comes from the work of Richard Parrot, Ph.D. and Terry Wardle, D.Min.

Journeying with Jesus involves both heart and mind. We can want to know God in Christ, want to live Christ-like lives, yet find ourselves significantly off course when we impose set ways of thinking and being. Incarnation is not an abstract activity; it is an act of embodiment in which we not only seek our being in Christ, but also allow God to act through us. Committing to the journey necessitates surrender and a willingness to step off known paths. This is why we begin by calibrating our compasses to Jesus' earthly journey. Just as in some parts of the word, there can be as much as a 25-degree difference between true north and magnetic north, so also there can be a variance between our understanding of who Jesus is and what scripture has to tell us about the One who is the way (John 14:6).

As Richard R. Niebuhr reminds us: "Pilgrims are persons in motion passing through territories not their own—seeking something we might call completion, or perhaps the word clarity will do as well, a goal to which only the spirit's compass points the way." When our lives are calibrated to core identity in Christ, we come to uncover what we really long for and thereby discover who we really are.

Journey Preparations
In addition to calibrating your compass to scripture, take some time now to note your present coordinates. I encourage you to do this by "drawing" a path of your life to date. Start with your birth at the bottom of the page and carry it up to the present moment, or collect images from magazines and newspapers and create a collage of your life journey.

What have you learned about yourself as you look at your life map? Do you see any patterns? Is there anything that has surprised you? Based upon your life map, what are your present coordinates?

Reflect on Jesus' life journey as illustrated with the itinerary from the prior section. What strikes you as the same? As different?

Spend some time in prayer, naming for God and yourself what you are hoping from this journey.

Prayer for the Journey
Where I wander—You!
Where I ponder—You again, always You!
You! You! You!
When I am gladdened—You!
When I am saddened—You!
Only You. You again, always You!
You! You! You!
You above! You below!
In every trend, at every end.
Only You. You again, always You!
You! You! You!
Levi Yitzchak of Beritchev

PACKING INSTRUCTIONS:
BE A PILGRIM, NOT A TOURIST

Isn't it time your drifting was consecrated into pilgrimage?
Alan Jones

All true journeys—all pilgrimages—begin with yearning. The journey to become like Jesus is born of a deep yearning to come home to God. Simple and profound, this yearning finds its roots in our remembering who and whose we are.

We, who are so often destination-bound, would do well to remember the call to be pilgrims, not tourists, on this life's journey. In the words of Suzanne Guthrie: "A tourist comes to see a place; a pilgrim comes to a holy place expecting to be changed. A pilgrim recognizes a holy landscape as a place mirrored within the soul." Such expectations open us to the transforming power of God.

As you prepare for this journey, pay attention to the changes going on inside yourself. Are there any places of resistance? Do you harbor any fears? Is there anything you need to let go of (or set aside for a season) in order to be fully present to the journey? How will you maintain your energy? How will you balance stress and renewal?

What will you pack? How we pack our bags often defines the journey. Are you going as tourist or pilgrim? Those who know me will tell you I travel light. My small roller bag is all I need to fit the essentials. I don't want to be bogged down by unnecessary luggage. The two non-negotiable items are my Bible and journal. With the advent of the iPad, I now carry my Bible in electronic form, along with a whole library. But my journal remains a leather-bound book. Writing longhand slows me down and helps me set aside preoccupations. Working on paper gives texture to my musings, and a leather journal does not need to be "powered down" during take offs and landings.

To be sure, going on pilgrimage involves courage. Deep down, we know that no journey is ever what we initially expect it to be. How much more so when we commit to journeying with Jesus! Missionary Hutson Smith believes that there are four key aspects to any pilgrimage: singleness of purpose, freedom from distraction, penance, and offering. Becoming like Jesus calls for singleness of purpose. Committing to the journey demands time set aside for freedom from distraction. Growing up in Christ will involve penance. The offering God asks of us is the gift of our very selves.

Are you a pilgrim or a tourist? Alan Jones, Dean Emeritus of Grace Cathedral, challenges, "Isn't it time your drifting was consecrated into pilgrimage? You have a mission. You are needed. The road that leads to no where has to be abandoned... It is a road for joyful pilgrims intent on the recover of passion" (qtd. in *The Art of Pilgrimage*, p. 26)

Are you ready? The Journey awaits!

Journey Preparations
People go on pilgrimage for many reasons: to visit a sacred space, to seek healing, to give thanks, to express their love for God, to heed an inner sense of call, to satisfy curiosity, or to reclaim a lost or abandoned part of oneself. Why are you considering this journey at this time? Below are some questions for reflection. Allow yourself some time to pause and ponder as you prepare for this journey.
1. How will you prepare for this journey?
2. Is there anything (activities, attitudes, other) that needs to be set aside in order to both free the time and allow you the space to commit to this journey?
3. What is calling you? Often pilgrimage begins with deep longing. Sometimes it is born out of a wounding. What is prompting you to consider making this journey at this time?
4. How do you need to prepare yourself to meet Jesus on this journey? What ritual actions might give expression to the desires of your heart?

Packing Instructions
I encourage you to pack light for this journey, bringing only that which is essential. There are two items that are non-negotiable: your compass (your Bible in a translation of your choice) and your journal. Without your compass, you will surely be lost. Your travel journal for journeying with Jesus will record your reflections on core identity, character, call and competence. There will be times when something will only make sense "later." Commit (even if you are not by nature one who journals) to daily reflecting on your journey. You will not regret it.

Prayer for the Journey

O God, who brought your servant Abraham out of the land of the Chaldeans, protecting him in his wanderings, who guided the Hebrew people across the desert, we ask that you watch over us, your servants, as we walk in the love of your name.

Be for us our companion on the walk, our guide at the crossroads, our breath in our weariness, our protection in danger, our refuge on the road, our shade in the heat, our light in the darkness, our consolation in our discouragements, and our strength in our intentions. So that with your guidance we may arrive safe and sound at the end of the Road and enriched with grace and virtue we return safely to our homes filled with joy.

In the name of Jesus Christ our Lord. Amen.

The Pilgrim's Mass

The Grace-Saturated Embrace

THE GRACE-SATURATED EMBRACE

In the fullness of time, God sent the Son.
Galatians 4:4

We live in a culture that rushes our growing up at great cost to both self and community. "The hurried child" is more than metaphor: it is a reality that results in "the lost adult." God never intended for us to grow up without the experience of the grace-saturated embrace. The divine embrace is God's means by which we come to know that we are loved and precious.

The importance of knowing who and whose we are cannot be understated. Only as we come to experience God's love in every fiber of our being will our core identity rest in Christ. Only then will we be ready for the challenges of the wilderness journey in which our characters are transformed. For those who were pressured to grow up quickly, this is an invitation to come home to the God.

Allow yourself the time and space to simply be with God. Enter into a season of "being" apart from the demands of "doing" so that you might learn anew what it is to be loved, celebrated, consecrated, and protected. Say yes to God's invitation to being formed in you!

Who we are matters! Too often, we confuse who we are with what we do. We do well to remember that call is, first and foremost, an invitation to wholeness born of relationship with the Triune God. Only then are we readied to complete the work of love that we are here to do.

As you begin this journey, know that the Lord God is with you, the One who takes great delight in you, in whose love there is no rebuke, but only rejoicing (Zephaniah 3:17).

Welcome to the journey!

ANNUNCIATION

Told of God's favor, told of God's purpose, Mary said yes...
Told of Christ Jesus, told of the Spirit,
can we say yes as Mary said yes?
Leach

Mary said yes. There are those who will argue that the angel wasn't asking, the angel was telling. Yet we are told that Gabriel waited for Mary's response. The angel—or rather, God through Gabriel—honored Mary's right to choose. It seems hard to imagine saying "no" to God. But if we're honest, we do it all the time, in big and little ways (mostly little, I think): those moments when we fail to acknowledge the movement of the Spirit within us, the times when we say no to bearing Christ through word and deed, choosing instead to care for ourselves, and never realizing the damage we do to ourselves and others.

Will we say yes to God? Before Christ can be formed in us, we must say yes. For many, this will involve a redefining of what it means to be a Christian: from a passive recipient to an active partner in the redemption of the world. We do well to ponder the challenge of 14th century mystic Meister Eckhart: "What good is it to me if the eternal birth of the Divine Son takes place unceasingly but does not take place within myself? And what good is it to me if Mary is full of grace if I am not also full of grace? What good is it for the Creator to give birth to his Son if I do not also give birth to him in my time and my culture? This then is the fullness of time, when the Son of God is begotten in us!"

In the words of Alan Hirsh and Michael Frost in The Shaping of Things to Come, an incarnational faith calls for acknowledgement of "the fact that in God's economy our actions do have eternal impact. We do extend the kingdom of God in daily affairs and activities and actions done in the name of Jesus." Annunciation announces God's in breaking into the world, through us! It is the proclamation of God's intent that Christ be formed in us, for the reconciliation of the world!

This then is the fullness of time, when the Son of God is begotten in us!

Will you say yes?

Food for the Journey
- Luke 1:26-38, The angel's visit to Mary

Journey Questions
1. In what ways have you said yes to the Son of God being begotten in you?
2. Are there any areas in your life that you haven't yielded? Can you name the source of your resistance? What stands in the way of saying yes to God?
3. How might God be calling you to bear Christ in this season of your life? What would be involved in allowing "the Son of God to be begotten in your time and your culture"?

Journey Practice: Interspersed Prayer

Any journey begins with saying yes. Given that, it is important that you understand to what you are saying yes. As you begin this formational journey, take some time to prayerfully ponder the invitation of God. Below is a prayer that intersperses the Annunciation with some suggestions for prayer and meditation. Allow yourself over this next week time for silence and solitude that the Word might enter and take root in you. Journey blessings as Christ is formed in you!

Before you begin, take a deep breath... and exhale. Now take another... and again release. Release any tension that you are carrying in your body. Release any expectation of what "should" happen in this time of prayer and yield yourself to God. Breathe... and release!

Prayer of Annunciation and Meditation

Greetings, O favored one! The Lord is with you! (Luke 1:28)
How does it feel to be favored in God's sight? What does it mean to know that the Lord is with you?

Do not be afraid, you have found favor with God. You will conceive and give birth (1:30-31).
What in the angel's greeting causes you fear? How do you receive these words of promise and assurance? In what way is God calling you to conceive and give birth to Emmanuel?

How will this be? (1:34)
What is your question of God?

The Holy Spirit will come upon you, and the power of the Most High will overshadow you… For no word from God will ever fail (1:35; 37).
Are you ready to yield to God, to surrender to the power of the Most High? What will it mean for God's Word to be born through you?

I am the Lord's servant… May it be to me according to your word (1:38).
Are you ready to say yes to God? If so, how will you embody this commitment in your life and living? If no, what stands in the way of your saying yes to God? What must you release or surrender in order to say yes?

Prayer for the Journey
God be with us as we seek to give birth to our souls.
As Mary carried you, may we carry our souls.
As your son was born,
may we give birth and life and form to your life and truth within us.
As Mary nourished and protected Jesus,
may we nourish and protect our inner life and our journey.
For our soul shall be our most painful birth, our most difficult child,
and the dearest gift we can give ourselves and our world.
Adapted from <u>A Common Prayer</u>

DREAMS

An angel of the Lord appeared to him in a dream.
Matthew 1:20

Dreams have been called God's forgotten language. Long before Jung wrote about the importance of dreams, God understood the power of the unconscious. Some sixteen chapters in the Hebrew scriptures and five chapters in the New Testament (in all, over seventy passages) share accounts of dreams and night visions in which God speaks into the lives (and living) of believers and skeptics alike. For Israel and the early church, dreams were one of the primary means by which God communicated: "I the Lord make myself known [...] in visions, I speak [...] in dreams" (Numbers 12:6).

The word "dream" is closely related to the Aramaic and Hebrew words "to be made healthy and strong." In Greek, the words to "dream" and the act of "dreaming" describe events, which are real, yet not originating in the external, physical world. Dreams are God's way of bringing the subconscious into the conscious. Often, dreams lead us to view reality in new ways.

This is especially true in the face of strong resistance. When heavily defended on a conscious level, God will often reach out on a subconscious level, speaking both love and challenge into our hearts and living. Dreams can challenge us to look at ourselves and understand our world in new ways. It is because of his dream that Joseph takes Mary as his wife.

Let us not forget that Joseph was a good man, a faithful man, well-versed in the traditions of his day. As Matthew tells us, Joseph was "a righteous man and did not want to expose Mary to public disgrace" (1:19). But nor did he want to marry a woman carrying another man's child! The betrayal was too deep. It was too much to expect of any man. And so, he decided to divorce her quietly.

How often do we, like Joseph, rationalize our actions? If we're honest, we take actions to protect our dignity and soothe our wounds. In human terms, Joseph's response to Mary's condition made sense. Nothing in his experience could have prepared him to understand that the child was indeed God's, that the Messiah was coming! That is what he and all of Israel prayed for. But, as a baby? Through the womb of his fiancé? Through him as earthly father? He had not signed on for this... yet!

Becoming Godbearers often takes some reorienting. Joseph, of the house and lineage of David, thought he understood what it meant to be a righteous man. His core values were shaped by the interpretation of the Torah in his day. The prescribed response for a woman having sex outside of marriage was death by stoning. While he could not bear the thought of Mary being killed, he was not ready for the radical reality of God breaking into the world. It took an angel of the Lord appearing to him in a dream to open him up to God's call.

How is God seeking to speak to you through your dreams? Is there some area of your life that, at least on a conscious level, is unavailable to God? Is there some part of your perspective in need of reorienting? You thought you understood. You thought you knew. But instead, do you find that inward and outward changes are being demanded of you? The formation of Christ within us will not come without letting go on our part. I have no doubt that Joseph's initial plans for his marriage differed from those of God. Is it possible that God has other plans for you and your life?

Food for the Journey
- Joel 2:28-32, The day of the Lord
- Acts 10:9-23, Peter's vision
- Matthew 1:18-25, The angel comes to Joseph in a dream

Journey Questions
1. Are there pockets of resistance in your life? If so, can you articulate the source of your resistance?
2. Can you name the deepest desire of your heart? Are you able to yield that desire to God? If not, what causes you to hold onto it?
3. Have you ever—or are you currently—encountering God in your dreams? What did you learn about God and about yourself?

Journey Practice: Journal Your Dreams
We live busy, full lives. Often, our conscious minds are distracted by the details of our daily living. Sometimes we are worried about what lies ahead. Other times, we are mired in the past. In the words of the poet, we are a people "distracted from distraction by distraction." Perhaps that is why God sometimes speaks to us in our dreams.

Journaling is first and foremost a way to help us remember our dreams. Many have found that if they don't write them down upon waking, they quickly evaporate from our consciousness.

This week, as you prepare for bed, place a pen and paper by your bedside. Pray that God will open your mind to the movement of the Holy Spirit as you dream. Ask God to speak to you upon waking and record what you remember. For some of us, it will take several weeks to develop the habit of remembering. But don't give up! Keep the pen and paper handy. Allow God to speak to you through your dreams and you will be blessed.

Prayer for the Journey
We give thanks for the darkness of the night where lies the world of dreams. Guide us closer to our dreams, so that they may nourish us. Give us good dreams and memory of them, so that they may carry their poetry and mystery into our daily lives. Grant us deep and restful sleep that we may wake refreshed with strength enough to renew a world grown tired. Let us restore the night and reclaim it as a sanctuary of peace, where silence shall be music to our hearts and darkness shall throw light upon our souls. Amen.
Michael Leunig, A Common Prayer

BIRTH IN THE SPIRIT

I was there to hear your borning cry; I'll be there when you are old.
I was there the day you were baptized to see your life unfold.
I was there when you were but a child, with a faith to suit you well;
In a blaze of light you wandered off to see where demons dwell.
John Ylvisaker, Borning Cry

What an amazing reality! God was there, present at our birth to hear our borning cry. Indeed, as the Psalmist reminds us: "All the days ordained for (us) were written in (God's) book before one of them came to be."(Psalm 139:16). We—each one of us—were created to be a masterpiece, God's *poiema*—God's work of art. But, for us to truly realize this reality, we must be born in the Spirit.

Now I don't know about you, but neither my pastor nor my Sunday school teachers ever told me that I needed to be born in the Spirit. Like the people in Ephesus, I knew what it was to be baptized into a baptism of repentance. Raised in a Reformed congregation, I knew about sin. But it was only later that I learned about the gift of the Spirit and the call to transformation.

Like Israel in the Valley of Dry Bones, I also needed to receive the breath of the Spirit. For me, that breath came in my valley. It was a gift born of yearning for purpose, for meaning, but most of all a yearning for God. The evangelist John tells us "God so loved the world that he gave his only Son that all who should believe in him should have eternal life" (3:16). But there is more to the story. As early church father Tertullian reminds us, "God became who we are that we might become what God is." But I'm getting ahead of myself. First, the delight. First, the joy. First, the grace-saturated embrace.

Just as any child loves to hear the story of his or her birth, so God loves for us to share in the story of his Son's birth. For in Jesus' birth, we will come to more fully understand our own birth in the Spirit and God's delight in us.

The Psalmist call us to "delight ourselves in the Lord, and God will give us the desires of our heart" (Psalm 37:4). In what do you delight? Are you ready to claim the power of the Holy Spirit that resides within you? Do you know that you are a temple of the Holy Spirit? Really? Yes, really!

To claim the Spirit's power can be unnerving, but it is a gift of God and the means by which we will grow up in Christ.

Food for the Journey
- Ezekiel 37:1-14, Valley of Dry Bones
- Acts 19:1-17, Baptism of the Holy Spirit
- I Corinthians 6:19-20, Temple of the Holy Spirit
- Matthew 1:18-25, The birth of Jesus

Journey Questions
1. Do you know the story of your baptism? If so, share it with a friend. If not, seek out those who will remember (even if you haven't spoken to them in years) and ask them to tell you the story of your baptism.
2. What does "birth in the Spirit" mean to you? How does scripture confirm or challenge your understanding?
3. What are the implications of receiving the Holy Spirit? What will this mean for your daily living?
4. Is there more learning involved? What would that entail?

Journey Practice: Remember Your Baptism
Martin Luther, who suffered from deep depression, had but one consolation: "I remember my baptism." Take some time to sit in silence and remember your baptism.

Reflect on the prayer below, an ancient baptismal prayer that has been said for hundreds of years over those who are about to be baptized or who are renewing their baptismal vows. Note how the first petition invites God to deliver us from our old life that has bound us to sin. The next three petitions (open, fill, keep) establish a new life pattern for the nurture and growth of the disciple. And the fifth and sixth petitions direct and enable ministry (teach, send). The final petition (bring) calls for the fullness of God's peace and glory.

As a means of inviting these actions of God to become the rhythm of our lives, make a daily practice of the next week of saying this prayer upon waking, at meal times and upon the close of day. As you pray this prayer, allow God to direct your thoughts and to lead you into further contemplation and prayer. Don't move onto the next petition until you are ready—or until the Spirit is ready!

You may also want to write the seven petitions on a small card that you can carry with you. Pray these petitions throughout the day. Be attentive and expectant to the leading the Spirit. (Source: David de Silva, *The Sacramental Life*.)

Prayer for the Journey
Deliver me, Lord, from the way of sin and death.
Open my heart to your grace and truth.
Fill with your holy and life-giving Spirit.
Keep me in the faith and communion of your holy Church.
Teach me to love others in the power of the Spirit.
Send me into the world to witness to your love.
Bring me to the fullness of your peace and glory.
Book of Common Prayer

COMMUNITY

Community will grow if we let it be more natural and spontaneous,
because the kingdom of heaven is like yeast. The yeast that comes to us
most spontaneously is natural friendship. The grace of God is with us
and we need to let it work. But we are slow to believe this.
Of course, sometimes it's quite hard to believe that grace is with us,
because there seems to be something in the system that wants to cage up
the Holy Spirit.
Thomas Merton, Seeds of Contemplation

Community comes in many forms, and not always in ways we can anticipate. I imagine that Mary expected to be in her home with her family surrounding her as she gave birth to her first child. But God had other plans. Instead of her mother and other kinsfolk, God provided an angelic host with shepherds and magi to celebrate Jesus' birth. There was the support of community, but not as anticipated. Dietrich Bonheoffer in Life Together reminds us that true community is God's grace: a gift to be received and treasured in whatever form it is given.

Our model for community is born out of the *perichoresis* (loosely translated, "the dance") of the Trinity. Just as Father, Son and Holy Spirit are one God, three persons, so we become most fully ourselves in the context of community. Mary was given much to ponder in her heart at the time of Jesus' birth. The community made known God's intent, although Jesus' calling as God's Son would not be fully understood until after his death and resurrection ("sing my song backwards!"). But the angels, the shepherds, the magi: all pointed to who Jesus was and would become.

At its best, Christian community provides the context in which we can grow up in God. In Christian community, we come to understand that we have been created for a purpose; that each one of us is called by God.

As a community of faith, we gather for worship, fellowship, study, and service. Anyone who has spent anytime in church (as with family) knows that community is messy. Whether we intend to or not, we bring the bad with the good as together we seek to be shaped and formed in the image of Christ. It takes a sustained effort to build community. But, more than that a, it takes a willingness to allow the Holy Spirit to be at work in our midst. To allow the leaven of the Spirit to nurture and grow our relationships. For then we come to see the face of Christ in one another and overcome the challenges that daily get in the way of being the body of Christ together.

We express God's nature best when we are part of a community committed to transforming degree by degree into the image of Christ.

Food for the Journey
- Ruth 1:16-22, Your people shall be my people
- Acts 2:42-47, The community of believers
- Luke 1:39-66, Mary and Elizabeth

Journey Questions
1. America has been called a "nation of cut-offs." We are "cut off" not only from one another but also from God. Do you agree or disagree?
2. How do you respond to the words: dependent, independent, and inter-dependent? How does your response affect your understanding and experience of Christian community?
3. When has the body of Christ nurtured and sustained you?
4. What gifts do you bring to community?

Journey Practice: The "One Anothers"
Write out the following "one another" verses on index cards (or print out the "one anothers" by accessing the PDF from the link in Appendix III).

Hand out the cards and ask the first person to read the "one another" command and place it on a table or floor. Then ask a second person to read, and place the card either above or below the pervious person's card depending upon which command they perceive the church obeys more readily. Continue until all cards have been played. Encourage conversation around the commands as they are played.

Note which commands are near the bottom and which are near the top. Why is that? Share your observations with one another and reflect on how the "one anothers" inform our understanding of community.

- Be at peace with one another. –Mark 9:50
- Love one another. –John 13:34; 15:12, 17; I John 3:11, 23; 4:7, 11, 12; II John 5
- Be devoted to one another and honor one another. –Romans 12:10
- Live in harmony with one another. –Romans 12:16; I Peter 3:8
- Stop passing judgment on one another. –Romans 14:13
- Accept one another, just as Christ accepted you. –Romans 15:7
- Instruct one another. –Romans 15:4

- When you come together to eat, wait for one another. –I Corinthians 11:33
- Have equal concern for each other. –I Corinthians 12:25
- Serve one another in love. –Galatians 5:13
- Be kind and compassionate, patient, bearing with one another. – Ephesians 4:32
- Speak to one another with songs, hymns, and spiritual songs.– Ephesians 5:19
- Forgiving one another. –Ephesians 4:32
- Submit to one another out of reverence for Christ. –Ephesians 5:21
- Teach (one another). –Colossians 3:13
- Do not lie to one another. –Colossians 3:9
- Admonish one another. –Colossians 3:16
- Encourage one another… daily. –I Thessalonians 5:11; Hebrews 3:13
- Spur one another on towards love and good deeds. –Hebrews 10:24
- Do not slander one another. –James 5:16
- Don't grumble against one another. –James 5:9
- Confess your sins to one another. Pray for one another. –James 5:16
- Clothe yourselves with humility toward one another. –I Peter 5:5

Prayer for the Journey
God of community, whose call is more insistent than ties of family or blood:
May we so respect and love those whose lives are linked to ours
That we fail not in loyalty to you, but make choices according to your will,
Through Jesus Christ. Amen.
Janet Morley, <u>All Desires Known</u>

CELEBRATION

May the Son of God who is already formed in you, grow in you,
so that for you, he will become immeasurable,
and that in you, he will become laughter, exaltation,
and the fullness of joy,
which no one can take away.
Isaac of Stella, 16th century Reformer

What a wonderful image –that the Son of God will become within us, with laughter, exaltation, and the fullness of joy! As people of resurrection, we are called to celebrate not in the absence of struggle or strife, but in the very midst of it. As Jeremiah, the most morose of prophets, reminds us, we are to celebrate even when our souls are downcast (Lamentations 3:20-24). Desert Father Abba Poemen put it this way: "The greater the hollow carved out in sorrow and grief, the more room for joy to dwell therein."

There is much to distract us from the joy that dwells therein. Yet Jesus came that his joy might be in us and that our joy might be full (John 15:11). How then do we prepare for such joy? How are we to welcome God into our hearts and lives? How do we celebrate the movement of the Holy Spirit in our midst?

John the Baptist calls us to repent. He does not want anything to get in the way of our meeting Christ when he comes again. Mary calls us to ponder the mystery of the Incarnation in our hearts. She knows that there are some truths, which cannot be explained in human terms, but must be trusted to God. Jesus, himself, calls us to wait for we know not when or where he will come. But that does not mean that we simply sit back and do nothing.

Like the shepherds and Magi, we too must seek out Jesus in daily living of our lives. Jesus, who enters our lives in the most unexpected of ways and places, calls us to be ready. With the angels, let us sing. With the shepherds and magi, let us bring our gifts: the sheep of our flock, the gold of our doxology, the frankincense of our meditation, and the myrrh of our sacrifice. But, most of all, as lambs of his flock, let us bring the gift of our very selves.

Celebration is a holy habit that must be nurtured and practiced as we "rejoice always [...] and give thanks in all circumstances" (II Thessalonians 5:16). Moses' sister Miriam understood the importance of celebration when she called Israel to singing and dancing in the face of God's mighty act of salvation. Celebration of God is not something to be saved for Christmas and Easter, for birthdays and anniversaries, but a way of being to be woven into the fabric of our lives that the Son of God might indeed become "laughter, exaltation and the fullness of joy."

Food for the Journey
- Exodus 15, The crossing of the Red Sea
- I Thessalonians 5:12-28, Rejoice always
- Luke 2:8-20; Matthew 2:1-12, Angels, shepherds, and Magi

Journey Questions
1. Where and when are you most prone to celebrate God? With others? During holidays or throughout the year? In worship? Alone? In nature? What does this tell you about how God made you?
2. Is there a part of you—an overly critical nature, seriousness, a wound—that gets in the way of your ability to celebrate God? How is God seeking to transform you in this area of your person and life?
3. Who do you know who really celebrates life and God? What can you learn from him or her?

Journey Practice: Nurturing Celebration
Below are three ways of nurturing the practice of celebration in your life:
1. Intentionally place yourself in the presence of God. Recall all of God's gifts, provisions, guidance and love around you. To celebrate God's grace with you, try a variety of methods: Write a psalm (a song) of praise and thanksgiving. Make a collage that represents your joy. Write a poem of praise, or play music and dance before the Lord. Memorize a verse of praise and repeat it throughout the coming days.
2. Name all the people in your life who have given you joy. Ask God how you might celebrate them in a way that honors and encourages them.
3. Consider how God loves you. Read Zephaniah 3:17. Then be still and listen. How is God celebrating you? Celebrate the God who celebrates you. Intentionally ask for the gift of appreciating yourself the way God does. (Source: Adele Ahlberg Calhoun, The Spiritual Disciplines Handbook)

Prayer for the Journey

This week, use the words of Isaac of Stella to bless both yourself and others. Inscribe the blessing below upon your heart as you celebrate this week!

May the Son of God who is already formed in me/you, grow in me/you—
so that for me/you, he will become immeasurable, and that in me/ you, he will become
laughter, exaltation, and the fullness of joy, which no one can take away.
Isaac of Stella

Ponder also "The Magi's Prayer":
My singing heart, my day's doxology, my gold, I bring for celebration.
My stillness, my glimpses of serenity, my frankincense, I bring for meditation.
My brokenness, my tears of sorrow, my myrrh, I bring for sacrifice.
Kate Compston, England, <u>Bread for Tomorrow</u>

CONSECRATION

Consecration means dedication to God. It occurs when we claim our deepest desire for God, beneath, above and beyond all other things. We may not understand the full meaning of consecration: the ups and downs, the joys and agonies of the journey that must follow. And certainly we will be unable to grasp the overarching cosmic meaning of our small assent, the joy it gives to God, the deepening love it will bring to humanity, the universal covenant it has enriched.
But our yes comes from some bare recollection of all these things. In a tiny space, our hearts can say yes.
Gerald May, Addiction and Grace

As was the custom, on the eighth day, Mary and Joseph brought Jesus to the temple that he might be consecrated unto the Lord (Luke 2:21-40). They were two parents presenting their first born to the Lord, dedicating him to serve God in some way. That was ordinary. This was done with all first-born, as a recognition that children came from the Lord and were entrusted to the parents by God's gift.

What wasn't ordinary was the child himself. The one being dedicated was God's Son—incarnate, conceived by the Holy Spirit, born of a virgin. What wasn't ordinary was that this holy child had been born without sin to take on the sin of the whole world—your sin, my sin. He entered our human situation, identifying fully with us, Emmanuel, God with us, that we might be saved. Jesus—the perfect sacrifice.

Mary and Joseph didn't even make it up the Temple steps before Simeon gave witness to God's intent: "Now let your servant depart in peace for these eyes of mine have seen the Savior whom you have prepared for all the world to see; a light to enlighten the nations and the glory of your people Israel" (verses 29-32). Quite a proclamation for an eight-day old child! But, as we know, Jesus was indeed God's light and our glory.

But, what of us? We too are called to be "the light of the world" and "salt of the earth" (The Sermon on the Mount, Matthew 5:13-16). Are we ready to consecrate our lives to God's purpose? Are we ready to acknowledge that we are called "to be holy" (Romans 1:7)? As Gerald May reminds us, "Consecration means dedication." It means that we desire God's will above our own. It means that we are ready to give our lives to God's purpose. Jesus' whole life was one of obedience. As 21st century Americans, we shy away from such demands. But, if we are to dedicate our lives to God, obedience to God's way and God's call is a necessary commitment.

At its root, obedience means "to hear" or "to listen towards." Simply put, obedience means to hear and obey God's Word. As Jesus is God's Incarnate Word, we are to hear and obey him. It begins with the Great Commandment to love the Lord with all our heart, soul, mind, and strength, even as we love our neighbors as ourselves (The Great Commandment in Mark 12:28-31). And our obedience is lived out as we grow up into maturity in Christ, being and making disciples (The Great Commission in Matthew 28:16-20). Is that tiny space in your heart ready to say yes? Are you ready to be consecrated unto the Lord?

Food for the Journey
- I Samuel 1:21-28, Consecration of Samuel
- Acts 9:1-19, Paul's conversion
- Luke 2:21-40, Jesus' consecration

Journey Questions
1. Ponder Gerald May's words in the heading quote. What response does it draw from you? What does your response tell you about your willingness to consecrate your life to God in Christ?
2. In many worship services, there is a prayer of dedication following the offering as we dedicate our tithes and gifts to God's purpose. What would it mean for us to dedicate not only our tithes and offerings but also our very selves to God?
3. How might you dedicate yourself and your life to God's service?

Journey Practice: Anointing
From the beginning of time, olive oil has been used to anoint in the name of God. In response to God's call, believers have used oil to set apart people, places, and even things to God's service. Use olive oil to anoint yourself, your family, and your home. As you do so, may you know yourself to be consecrated to God, set apart for God's work.

Prayer for the Journey
Take, Lord, and receive all my liberty,
my memory, my understanding, and my entire will.
All I have and call my own.
Whatever I have or hold, you have given me.
I return it all to you and surrender it wholly

45

to be governed by your will.
Give me only your love and your grace
and I am rich enough and ask for nothing more.
Ignatius of Loyola

PROTECTION

I arise today. Christ with me, Christ before me,
Christ behind me, Christ in me,
Christ beneath me, Christ above me,
Christ on my right, Christ on my left,
Christ when I lie down, Christ when I sit down, Christ when I arise,
Christ in the heart of everyone who thinks of me,
Christ in the mouth of everyone who speaks of me,
Christ in every eye that sees me, Christ in every ear that hears me.
I arise today through a mighty strength, the invocation of the Trinity,
Through belief in the threeness,
through confession of the oneness, of the Creator of Creation.
St. Patrick's Breastplate, 8th c., Ireland

The angel came to Joseph in a dream (again!): "Get up," the angel said, "take the child and his mother and escape to Egypt. Stay there until I tell you, for Herod is going to search for the child to kill him" (Matthew 2:13). And Joseph did as he was told. While Jesus was Savior from the beginning, his time had not yet come. Like Moses before him, Jesus needed protection so he might grow up "and become strong; filled with wisdom, and the grace of God" (Luke 2:40). Joseph and Mary, along with extended family, were given the task of ensuring his safety and providing for his care.

The protection afforded to Jesus prompts a question: In what ways are we to provide "protection" for those new to the faith that they too might grow up in wisdom and grace? How do we provide for the nurture and care of not only our children, but also all who seek to grow up in Christ?

There is a petition in Compline (the final Office of the day) that haunts me. It calls upon God to "shield the joyous." That is, to allow for a season of delight, to not rush the journey or hasten the growing up that will surely come. For everything there is a season, and for those new or returning to the faith (or even at one of life's crossroads), it is important for us to protect and shield them... and even ourselves!

Protect from what, you ask? Serving in ways that God has never called us to serve. Triangles born of petty conflicts that have nothing to do with a newfound love of God. Cynicism that gets in the way of delight. Anything and everything that might prevent one from experiencing the joy born of knowing and loving God. As Abba Elias said, "If the spirit does not sing with the body, labor is in vain."

47

Joy is a precious gift, easily overturned by responsibilities and expectations that we and others place upon us. So, next time a new face appears in the pews, don't immediately think of what they can do for the church. Rather, ask how God might be calling you to "shield the joyous." How might you help them (and yourself) to become more fully aware of the Christ who dwells with us, before us, beneath us, ahead of us? How might you protect them from that which will get in the way of their love affair with God?

Food for the Journey
- Exodus 2:1-10; 11-25, Moses' birth/Moses flees to Midian
- Galatians 5:1-21, Fruit of the Spirit
- Matthew 2:13-18, The Flight to Egypt

Journey Questions
1. Can you think of a time when the "work of the church" got in the way of your relationship with God? How did you protect your relationship with God?
2. What in you, in this season, needs to be protected and nurtured? Who will help to protect your relationship with God?
3. What is God calling you to protect in another? How might you "shield the joyous"?

Journey Practice: Margins
It is not likely that we will protect others if we do not first learn to protect ourselves. Augustine believed "Our hands are too full to receive the good that God desires to give us." The challenge, it appears, is not to discern between "good" and "bad," but rather to discern between "good" and "faithful." Jesus' strong injunction is to "let our yes be yes and our no be no" (Matthew 5:37).

Dr. Richard Swenson, in his book Margin, believes that we live margin-less lives. In order to create margins, he challenges us to cut out all unnecessary activities. He further challenges us to scale back on commitments. We do well to ask ourselves, "Is this essential? Is it of God?"

In order to restore balance and health, we need to have "margins." We need to have balance between being and doing, between stress and renewal. Only then will we know the wholeness born of balance; only then will we nurture a capacity for deep joy. That said, discernment as to how to develop margins (and then maintain them) can be hard. Jesus models a way through time apart with God. Even when it involved getting up before dawn, Jesus knew he could not faithfully discern his margins unless he had time in silence and solitude. This next week, consider getting up ten minutes earlier to be with God at the start of the day. Allow that time to shape your response to the demands you encounter throughout the day.

Prayer for the Journey
Ignatius of Loyola believes that sin is unwillingness to trust that what God wants for us is our deepest happiness. Can you pray the prayer below?

Lord, I am willing to receive what you give,
release what you take, lack what you withhold,
do what you require, and be who you desire. Amen.
Adele Ahlberg Calhoun, <u>The Spiritual Disciplines Handbook</u>

GROWTH IN THE SECRET PLACE

If then you are wise, you will show yourself rather as a reservoir than as a canal. A canal spreads abroad the water as it receives it, but a reservoir waits until it is filled before overflowing, and thus without loss to itself communicates its superabundant water.
Bernard of Clairvaux, <u>Sermons on the Songs</u>, 18:2

Our formation in Christ is not to be rushed. Moses spent forty years as a nomadic shepherd. While a Pharisee among Pharisees, Paul also needed time apart in Arabia to nurture his newfound faith in Christ. Even Jesus himself did not begin his public ministry until he was thirty. He spent his years in Egypt and in Nazareth in relative obscurity coming to know God and God's people.

Many of us, however, do not know how to be alone. We confuse solitude (growth in the secret place) with loneliness. Often, it takes challenge and chaos to bring us to the secret place where we may come to know ourselves for who we are in Christ.

Moses, having killed an Egyptian, was literally running for his life. Paul, as a result of his conversion, was trusted by neither Jew nor Christian. Had Mary and Joseph remained in Bethlehem, Jesus would have been among those slaughtered.

But solitude and loneliness are not the same. One of the primary functions of solitude is to settle us into God. Where loneliness is inner emptiness, solitude is inner fulfillment. Each of us needs time alone—time apart from our busy lives—in order that we might come to know our God and find ourselves. Only when our lives are rooted in Christ will we have something to give others. As a monk from the Abbey of Genesee put it, "The measure of our solitude is the measure of our capacity for communion."

When we dare to allow ourselves time for growth in the secret place, we find ourselves freed to become the very people God created us to be. We are able to surrender our limitations and our fear, even as we take hold of the reality that we are fearfully and wonderfully made.

Only through time apart in "the secret place" will our lives come to be like reservoirs feeding from their overflow. Yet, far too many of us live lives like canals that run until they grow dry. We never come to know our true selves. We never come to know the power of God within us.

There is a desperate need in our times for spiritual depth born of growth in the secret place.

Food for the Journey

- Exodus 2:11-22, Moses, an alien in a foreign land
- Galatians 1:11-24, Paul in Arabia following his conversion
- Matthew 2:13-18, Jesus in Egypt

Journey Questions

1. Why do you think "growth in the secret place" was necessary for Moses, Paul and Jesus to live into God's call?
2. What would "growth in the secret place" look like for you? What shape might solitude—time apart with God—take in your life?
3. How might the expectation of growth in the secret place be woven into the expectations of your church family as you challenge one another to become like "reservoirs"?

Journey Practice: Your Secret Place

Your journey into the secret place need not be as dramatic at that of Moses, Paul, or Jesus. The impetus might simply be a longing that just won't go away—a sense of missing God—which all the accolades of ministry cannot fill. It might be a level of exhaustion that no one else knows about—yet! It might be an awareness of a sin pattern that you used to be able to control but now is pressing in on you with greater urgency. It might be feelings of hopelessness or depression that no one else sees, yet a dark current is crossing under the surface of your busy life, threatening to pull you under. It doesn't really matter how the invitation comes. What matters is that you say yes.

Take a few moments now to sit quietly in God's presence and notice what it is that is drawing you into growth in the secret place. Try not to fight the awareness of need that comes or talk you out of solitude. If, like Moses, what you see causes you to be afraid, let yourself experience that fear. If, like Paul, you feel the need to deepen your relationship with God in preparation for heeding God's call, allow you the time apart with God. If, like Jesus, God seeks to protect and nurture you in this season, receive the gift (Adapted from Ruth Haley Barton, *Strengthening the Soul of Your Leadership*).

Prayer for the Journey

Circle me, Lord, keep protection near and dangers afar.
Circle me, Lord, keep hope within and doubt without.
Circle me, Lord, keep lights near and darkness afar.
Circle me, Lord, keep peace within and evil out.
David Adams, The Edge of Glory

RETURN TO NAZARETH

We shall not cease from exploration
And the end of all our exploring
Will be to arrive where we started
And know the place for the first time.
T.S. Eliot, "Little Gidding" (the last of his Four Quartets)

It has been said that you can't go home. Yet, the journey (by necessity) calls us home that we might know ourselves, often for the first time. For many of us, this involves reclaiming parts of our past that we might become whole.

Once again, an angel comes to Joseph in a dream to tell him that it is safe to take Mary and Jesus home. By that time, he would have been about seven years old. Of course, Jesus had never been to Nazareth. But his roots were there. It was home to Mary and Joseph. The Nazareth of Jesus' day was a very, very small place. Secluded. Population estimated at 100. It was a safe place in which to raise the Son of God.

Just as Egypt had provided protection against Herod the Great, so Nazareth provided protection from his son, Herod Antipas. While only 64 miles north of Jerusalem, Nazareth was in a different province and as such did not fall under his jurisdiction. It was a place where Jesus could grow up with the support of extended family and community.

Nazareth allowed him to have the freedoms of childhood not afforded in a city center. It "rooted" him, allowing him to know where he came from and whose he was. Much like the African notion of "Ubuntu," Jesus would have learned in Nazareth about the inter-connectedness of community. As Bishop Desmond Tutu notes, Ubuntu teaches us: "You can't be human all by yourself, and when you have this quality – Ubuntu – you are known for your generosity. We think of ourselves far too frequently as just individuals, separated from one another, whereas you are connected and what you do affects the whole world."

In Western culture, in particular, we have developed a flawed notion that we can define ourselves as individuals apart from community. Our "Nazareths" help us to know and claim our full selves. It is then we come to understand what the apostle Paul meant when he wrote: "So, in Christ we, though many, form one body, and each member belongs to all the others" (Romans 12:5).

Do you know your Nazareth? Can you name your roots?

Food for the Journey
- Exodus 2:1-10, The birth of Moses
- Romans 12:3-8, Humble service in the Body of Christ
- Luke 2:39-40, Christ grows in strength and wisdom

Journey Questions:
1. Do you have a Nazareth? What roots do you need to give thanks for?
2. Is there a part of you that needs to be reclaimed? How might you begin?
3. How does Jesus' childhood inform your understanding of your spiritual journey?

Journey Practice: Roots
Appalachian poet George Ella Lyon's poem, "Where I'm From," speaks to the power of roots. As Jan Richardson writes: Lyon "provides a rich litany of places and people, artifacts and experiences that holds the poet's roots in a profound way." The opening stanza begins with:

I am from clothespins,
From Clorox and carbon-tetrachloride,
I am from the dirt under the back porch.
(Black, glistening, it tasted like beets.)

This week, take some time to journal about your own roots, pondering the places, people, and experiences that have shaped your journey. Author Jan Richardson asks: "What holds your roots? How does where you're from help you understand who you are? How does your past help you find the path ahead?"

Consider writing your own "Where I'm From" poem. Claim your roots.

Prayer for the Journey
Blessed be the people we carry in our blood.
Blessed be the places we carry in our bones.
May our living make a way for those who come after;
A path of blessing, a path of beauty.
Jan Richardson

IN THE TEMPLE

Holiness, as taught in the scriptures, is not based upon knowledge on our part. Rather, it is based upon the resurrected Christ in-dwelling us and changing us into his likeness.
A.W. Tozer

Jesus is in "his Father's house." It is, for him, a holy place where he knows he belongs. The political realities that will later lead to his arrest and crucifixion are not yet pressing in. One can imagine a bright and somewhat precocious youth, both learning from the teachers while also delighting them with his wisdom. Those who hear him, marvel.

We all need holy places in our lives: places where our elders delight in us; safe places where we can bring our questions and share our insights. The Temple provided Jesus with an extended community, beyond his family, to press his questions. Sometimes our families are not ready to release us from the protection of the grace-saturated embrace. With the best of intentions, they hold on too tight.

Growing up is not without its challenges, even for the Son of God. Even the most loving of families can struggle with the growing independence that comes with adolescence. But Jesus is ready to learn and grow. He seeks both inspiration and confirmation of his deepest intuitions. One senses that he is becoming aware of who he is. He is beginning to see the world through different eyes.

This question of "Who am I?" is one that we each must experience if we are to grow up into maturity in Christ. This is not a question that can be answered by studying a book. It is something we come to know in the context of relationship, through the modeling of others, and the testing of our inward thoughts as they are put into action. Jesus knew that he needed to be "in his Father's house." It was a safe place in which he could "increase in wisdom and favor with God and people" (Luke 2:52).

On your journey, have you had a holy place—a temple—where you could go to live your questions? Who have been the people to mentor and encourage you on the journey?

Food for the Journey

- Proverbs 8:32-36, Wisdom's call
- Ephesians 3:14-21, A prayer for the Ephesians
- Luke 2:41-52, The boy Jesus in the Temple

Journey Questions

1. Take some time to remember your faith as both a child and an adolescent. If you attended church, what do you remember about the people, the building, and the experience of going to church? What role did church play in your growing up and faith formation? Were there wise people to guide you?
2. Who was God to you as a child? Has your image of God changed in any way as you have grown older? How did you pray, then and now?
3. Who was involved in your faith development? What did you learn from them? Who is involved in your faith development now?

Journey Practice: At the Feet of Jesus

In the temple, the boy Jesus sat at the feet of the teachers, listening to them and asking them questions (Luke 2:46). Read through Luke 2:41-52 several times. Allow your attention to be drawn to the different individuals in the passage. In this season, do you feel more like the teachers who are busy instructing, or Mary and Joseph, anxiously looking for Jesus? Or do you feel like Jesus himself, at home "in his Father's house"? In what season of your life have you felt most "at home in your Father's house"? Take some time over this next week to place yourself at the feet of Jesus. Listen deeply for what Jesus has to say to you in this season.

Prayer for the Journey

Take time over the next week to pray Paul's prayer found in Ephesians 3:14-21, both for yourself and those whom God places on your heart:

I pray that out of God's glorious riches, he may strengthen (me/others by name) with power through his Spirit in (my/your) inner being, so that Christ may well in (my/your) hearts through faith. And I pray that (I/you) being rooted and established in love, may have power, together with all the Lord's people to grasp how wide and long and high and deep is the love of Christ, and to know that this love surpasses knowledge—that (I/you) may be filled with the measure of the fullness of God. Now to the One who is able to do immeasurably more than we ask or imagine, according to his power at work within us, to him be glory in the church and in Christ Jesus throughout all generations, forever and ever! Amen.

The Journey:
Growing Up in Christ

Love & Testing

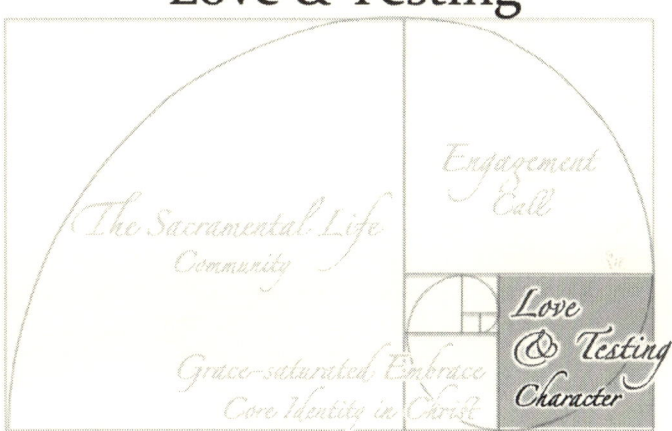

LOVE AND TESTING

And what do you benefit if you gain the whole world
but lose your own soul?
Is anything worth more than your soul?
Matthew 16:26, NLT

This next movement of the journey involves love and testing. With Jesus, we enter the wilderness that our characters might be transformed. While the formational journey begins with the grace-saturated embrace, we will not continue to grow apart from testing. Much as we shy away from the pain, it is the means by which Christ-like virtues take deep root in us.

Try as we might, not one of us can avoid this piece of the journey. There is no immunity from pain or suffering. The question is how will we respond? Will we allow the wilderness experiences to become crucibles in which all that is not of Christ is burned away? Will we allow our wounds to be healed and characters refined? Or will we hold onto our pain, projecting the residue of our failures onto both self and others, remaining stuck in a place of immaturity? The compass needle points us in a direction we would rather not go, yet it is essential if we are to become like Jesus.

While this part of the journey begins with confirmation of the Father's love on the riverbank, the Spirit quickly drives us into the wilderness. Taken together, love and testing are the means by which we are prepared for the challenges of call that lie ahead. We do well to attend to this part of the journey. To neglect this path is to risk losing our soul.

As Jesus asks, "Is anything worth more than your soul?"

DUST AND DELIGHT

I was there when you were but a child, with a faith to suit you well;
In a blaze of light you wandered off to find where demons dwell.
John Ylvisaker

Dust and delight! That is what we are made of. Dust from the ground of creation; delight from the heart of the Father. God breathed life into *Ádamah* ("the stuff of the ground"), and we took form. And God said, "It is good—very good!"

When child is born, there is delight, and everyone says, "It is good—very good!" Such is the joy of the grace-saturated embrace. But the time comes for us all when we must wander off to find where demons dwell. Each and every one of us must confront the darkness within and without. It is then we find ourselves in the wilderness. This is the context in which our character is transformed by challenge and testing. Thankfully, such is the depth of God's love that we are not expected to heed God's call without first being prepared.

For most of us, it takes a firm push to move us into the wilderness—a disruption, or life throws us a curve ball we didn't anticipate. There is an unexpected loss. What worked no longer works. Whatever form "the push" takes, we are brought face to face with our fears, our insecurities, and personal frailties. Only as they are made known can we learn and grow from them.

Jesus' wilderness time brought him face to face with three temptations: hunger, power, and safety. The wilderness confronts each one of us with the reality that our hunger cannot be satisfied by bread alone; we need God. Nor will power insulate us from life's challenges; we need God. Nor will we avoid the pain of failure by seeking protection against risk; we need God. The invitation of the wilderness is to align ourselves with God's ways, so that we are then able to discern between true life and false seductions. Yet the question of the wilderness remains: Will we become the people we were created to be, even knowing that there will be pain and challenge and failure?

The ancient liturgy reminds us that we are dust and to dust shall we return. It can sound ominous, unless we remember that returning to the dust inevitably means returning home to God. The Divine embrace awaits us and in that embrace is delight even in the face of loss and failure. Such is

DEBORAH ANNE RUNDLETT

the paradox of faith: the greater the hollow carved out by challenge, the more room for joy to dwell therein.

May we dare to embrace the wilderness journey in which love and testing will both refine and remind us of who and whose we are.

Food for the Journey
- Genesis 2:4-7, God forms us from the dust
- I Corinthians 15:35-58, The first man was of the dust, the second man is of heaven
- Matthew 11:28-30, Come to me

Journey Questions
1. The Latin word for "earth" is *humus*, from which our word humility comes. In essence, humility is to be "earthed" in God that we might acquire true self-knowledge: knowledge of who we are in Christ, knowledge of where we have fallen short. In what ways are you "earthed" in God? In what ways have you disconnected from the terrain of the formational journey?
2. It has been said that our rebirth in integrity takes time and many repentances. Of what do you need to repent in order to be "earthed" anew in God? Take some time to look beyond behavior patterns to the disposition of your heart and soul. Being "earthed" makes no sense apart from seeking to become one with Jesus, who describes himself as being "meek and humble of heart."
3. What in you resists heeding Jesus' invitation in Matthew 11:28-30 to come to him? Are you able to name why?

Journey Practice: Resting in Jesus
Menuha is the Hebrew word for "rest." Loosely translated, *menuha* means to "catch our breath." Over time, the failure to stop, "catch our breath" and breathe in the Breath of Life results in spiritual death. From the beginning, physical breath and spiritual breath have been intimately linked. God breathed into Adam's nostrils the breath of life and he lived. Even now, God seeks to fill each one of us with that same breath of life. This week, take some time to stop and "catch your breath."

A recent survey of 20,000 Christians around the world revealed that busyness and constant overload is a major obstacle to "catching our breath." We have become enslaved to busyness. We live in bondage to overload. A diagnosis of our condition (according to John Ortberg) reveals:

60

- Hurry sickness: Perhaps best explained by Lewis Carroll, "said the Red Queen to Alice: 'Now here, you see, it takes all the running you can do, to keep in the same place. If you want to get somewhere else you must run at least twice as fast.'";
- Multi-tasking: The illusion that we can do more than one thing at a time;
- Clutter: All of our "stuff" (including the time-saving gadgets and books we don't have time to read) reflects a lack of simplicity;
- Superficiality: The curse of our age. We need to exchange depth for breadth;
- An inability to love: Relationships take time, and hurry doesn't allow time;
- Sunset fatigue: Giving our loved ones the "leftovers of our energy," always rushing, short tempered, loss of gratitude and wonder, indulging in self-destructive habits, including too much food and drink, TV, not enough time with God, others, and self.

How would diagnose your present state? Do you know how to rest in Jesus?

Prayer for the Journey
Ponder Jesus' invitation below:

Come to me. Get away with me and you'll recover your life. I'll show you how to take a real rest. Walk with me and work with me—watch how I do it. Learn the unforced rhythms of grace. I won't lay anything heavy or ill-fitting on you. Keep company with me and you'll learn to live freely and lightly.
Matthew 11:28-30, The Message

THE POTTER'S HAND

It is not you who shape God; it is God who shapes you. If then you are the work of God, await the hand of the Artist who does all things in due season. Offer the Potter your heart, soft and tractable, and keep the form in which the Artist has fashioned you. Let your clay be moist, lest you grow hard and lost the imprint of the Potter's fingers.
Irenaeus

I have always been startled by how brittle clay becomes when left unattended. That which is moist and yields to touch quickly dries out unless it is kept damp and protected from the drying effects of the air. No longer is it soft and tractable, no longer is the artist able to fashion a work of art. The clay instead becomes hardened and brittle in its half-finished state.

When we resist the path of love and testing, we lose the imprint of the Potter's hand. We too become brittle to touch. The moistness born of the grace-saturated embrace is lost and we begin to crumble. Often, our resistance is born of knowing that the Refiner's fire follows the hand of the Artist. Authenticity, honesty, integrity are qualities that can only be fully forged in the crucible of the wilderness. Testing is the context in which God seeks to convict and heal us, degree by degree, that we might be transformed into the image of Christ (II Corinthians 3:17-18). We each bring wounds. We all have sinned. But only one sin is unredeemable: to not learn from our mistakes.

Hard as it is to admit, our times of greatest growth are often born out of challenge. Dark times nourish and shape our souls in ways that the grace-saturated embrace cannot, even as the testing prepares us for the challenges that lie ahead. To be sure, both paths are needed if we are to become like Jesus. Without the grace-saturated embrace, we will never fully know the reality that we are beloved of God, "fearfully and wonderfully made" (Psalm 139:14). But without testing, our characters will remain undeveloped. We risk confusing who we are with what we do. We will not be prepared for the challenges that lie ahead.

We live in a world where pain abounds. Our lives are shaped as much by loss as by gain. Sorrow is interwoven with joy. The wilderness is the place where we come to acknowledge our shadows, name temptation, and embrace pain that we might fully claim who we are in Christ. It is the place where we are invited to yield to God all that is false so our characters might be transformed. This is the means by which God nurtures compassion and embodies hope for the journey that lies ahead.

As we embark on this part of the journey, may we offer the Potter our hearts, soft and tractable, and thereby keep the form in which the Artist has fashioned us.

Food for the Journey
- Jeremiah 18:1-6, The Potter God
- Psalm 139, Fearfully and wonderfully made
- II Corinthians 4:7-9, Jars of clay

Journey Questions
1. When have you felt most "moist" to the Potter's hand? What practices or holy habits helped to keep you "soft and tractable"?
2. Have you ever lost the imprint of the Potter's hand? What circumstances led to your losing "the form in which the Artist had fashioned you"?
3. In what ways have you been refined by the Refiner's fire? How has that shaped your character and sense of call?

Journey Practice: Reflecting on the Steps to Make Pottery

Step 1: A potter first must clean it to make it usable. Raw clay is washed in large pots called blungers to remove pebbles and sand. *What core practice would you see paralleling this first step?*

Step 2: Clay is moistened to make it more flexible and easier for the potter to hand. *What helps you to keep your heart—your clay—soft and tractable to the Potter's hand?*

Step 3: The next step is to actually form the object. "Throwing" a piece of clay onto the potter's wheel to spin it that it might be shaped and formed often does this. *How is God seeking to shape and form you? What in you must cease in order for this to happen? What in you must begin in order for this to happen?*

Step 4: After the object is shaped, it is ready for firing in a kiln at either 1700°F for pottery or 2700°F for porcelain. *In what way does God seek to purify you with the Refiner's Fire?*

Step 5: There are many different kinds of glazes. Under glaze decoration (the design) is painted on after first firing. Then it is glazed before the second firing. *What strengths has God given you that set you apart for a particular ministry? How are you using/not using those gifts?*

Prayer for the Journey
Spirit of the Living God, fall afresh on me.
Spirit of the Living God, fall afresh on me.
Melt me, mold me, fill me, use me.
Spirit of the Living God, fall afresh on me.
Traditional Hymn

BEHOLD, THE LAMB OF GOD!

Behold, the Lamb of God who takes away the sins of the world!
John the Baptist

Jesus' entry into public ministry begins on the muddy riverbank of the Jordan.

Site of Israel's crossing over into the Promised Land, the Jordan River is now used by John the Baptist to provide a new beginning for those in bondage to their sin and brokenness. It provides confirmation of the Father's love for Jesus as he begins his public ministry (Luke 3:1-22). Tiny in size, the waters of the Jordan become the waters of new life for all who feel burdened by their sin and overcome by their brokenness. John offers them something previously only available to new converts: a baptism of repentance.

Quoting from Isaiah, John refers to himself as "the voice of one crying in the wilderness" (Isaiah 40:3; Luke 3:4-6). And cry he did, calling sinners to confess their sins and be baptized. He is described by the gospels in stark terms. Matthew tells us that John wore a garment of camel's hair with a leather girdle around his waist. His eating habits were also odd, with a diet that consisted of locusts and wild honey. Yet people flocked to him, seeking release from their brokenness and pain. Even Jesus sought him out and, although John protested, was baptized by him.

John protested because he knew who Jesus was: "Behold the Lamb of God who takes away the sins of the world" (John 1:29). Luke tells us that John knew who Jesus was even before he was born, leaping in his mother's womb for joy when Elizabeth embraced her cousin Mary (1:41). Now they meet again, and this time the setting is the River Jordan, a place of healing and new beginnings.

Later, when John was in prison facing death, he will send his disciples to ask Jesus: "Are you the One who is to come, or are we to look for another?"(Matthew 11:1-19). Could John really have doubted Jesus? As he faced death, had he really come to question the validity of Jesus' ministry? Jesus' response was to tell John's disciples to look around: the sick are healed, the blind given sight, the disenfranchised given hope. What did they think? What did John think?

John's question is one which we all must ask as we make the journey: Are you the One? Only in the asking will we come to claim the answer for ourselves. Just as John's question came to him in the midst of trial, so this question will be put before us in our time of challenge.

Who is Jesus to you? Will you permit him to accompany you on your wilderness journey? Will you allow his journey to inform your journey?

On Jordan's bank, the Baptist's cry announces that the Lord is nigh!

Food for the Journey
- Isaiah 40:1-5, The Voice of one crying out in the wilderness
- Acts 2:14-41, Cut to the heart
- Luke 3:1-22, John the Baptist prepares the way

Journey Questions
1. Do you find it easy or hard to repent? Why is that?
2. What is your experience of the discipline of confession? How does this inform or challenge your understanding of the wilderness path?
3. In times of trial and challenge, who is Jesus to you?

Journey Practice: Confession of Faith
Reformer John Calvin described the Psalms as "the anatomy of all parts of the soul." He approached prayer with an honesty and candor that leaves many of us feeling uncomfortable and exposed. Like the psalmist, Calvin cut right to the heart of prayer giving answer to God out of every part of his being. When we dare to approach God with the same candor, we find both body and soul are made whole. When we are truly honest about both our feelings and our actions, we come to accept ourselves for who we really are and thereby find ourselves opened up to the healing hand of God at work in our lives.

Psalm 51 is David's confession following his adultery with Bathsheba. Though he was a man after God's own heart, he had failed both God and his people. Yet even in this deep place of pain, he never loses his voice for praise. Confession is often associated with the naming of sins. As with the psalmist, we pray that God will have mercy on us and create in us a new heart. But, that is only part of our confession.

Confession, if it is to be complete, includes our praise: "Open my lips and my mouth will proclaim your praise." Just as we confess our sins, so also we are called to "confess" that Jesus is Lord. Over this next week, write a Psalm in which you both confess to God your sin and your praise.

Prayer for the Journey
God help us to find our confession;
The truth within us which is hidden from our mind;
The beauty or the ugliness we see elsewhere but never in ourselves;
The stowaway which has been smuggled into the dark side of the heart;
Which puts the heart off balance and causes it pain, Which wearies and confuses us,
Which tips us in false directions and inclines us to destruction,
The load which is not carried squarely because it is carried in ignorance.
God help us to find our confession. Help us across the boundary of our understanding.
Lead us into the darkness where we can find what lies concealed;
That we may confess it towards the light;
That we may carry our truth in the center of our heart; That we may carry our cross wisely and bring harmony into our life and our world. Amen.
–Michael Leunig, A Common Prayer

ENTERING THE MESS

To be open to the embrace of the Father is necessarily and inevitably
to be open to the whole creation, which is held in his embrace.
Brother Martin Smith, SSJE

Have you ever wondered why Jesus chose to enter the mess? He didn't have to. He could have kept his distance, looking down from afar upon the crowd who had flocked out to John seeking forgiveness for their sins. He who was without sin could have stood at a distance, not getting caught up in the chaos. Yet on that riverbank, he makes the conscious choice to enter the fullness of our condition.

It is in that precise moment that God's pleasure can no longer be contained: "This is my beloved Son with whom I am well pleased" (Matthew 2:22). Take note of the Father's joy as the Son throws away his separateness to enter into our brokenness. He who is without sin becomes one with us in our pain. It is then that the Spirit descends, filling him with an awareness of his true identity as the beloved Son. Only as Jesus heeds God's call to take on our suffering does God flood him with awareness of his unique relationship as the only-begotten Son and anoint him with the Spirit for his mission; not before. It is the same for us. Only as we step out in faith will we receive confirmation of our core identity in Christ and God's call.

When Jesus chose to plunge himself that day into our condition, he revealed that nothing shall separate us from the love of God (see Romans 8:31-39). What a profound moment of truth for us! In his baptism, Jesus embodies God's love for us even as he challenges us to follow him into the mess. From the prophets on, God has called us to seek the Shalom of the cities to which we have been sent in exile (see Jeremiah 29:1-11). Jesus models this with his baptism as he enters into our brokenness.

This is the axis on which the gospel turns. The same movement of surrender that opens us to intimacy with God also opens us up to compassion with all who struggle and are in need. To be open to the Spirit is to be open to humanity in all its brokenness and its ardent yearning for wholeness.

As Brother Martin Smith of the Society of Saint John the Evangelist reminds us: "To be open to the embrace of the Father is necessarily and inevitably to be open to the whole creation, which is held in his embrace."

Food for the Journey
- Jeremiah 29:1-11, Seek the Shalom of the city to which I have sent you in exile
- Romans 8:31-39, Nothing shall separate us from the love of God
- Matthew 3:13-17, Jesus' baptism

Journey Questions
1. Just as God's pleasure could no longer be contained when Jesus entered into our broken humanity, so God's pleasure is made known in us when we bear his heart into a suffering world. In what ways have you born Christ's heart into the world?
2. What commitments are you ready to make with regard to the shaping of your character that you might be ready for this journey?
3. Are you ready to enter the mess? Are you ready to allow your life to run on the same axis as Jesus, an axis that led to betrayal and death?

Journey Practice: Entering the Mess
Read through the four accounts of Jesus baptism: Matthew 3:1-17; Mark 1:1-8; Luke 3:1-37; John 1:19-34. Do not try to reconcile the differences in the four accounts, receive them for their different perspectives, each offering revelation. Now, choose one account and read it aloud. Take a moment to ponder the scene again. Where are you on that muddy riverbank? Are you part of the crowd? One of John's disciples? John the Baptist? Jesus, himself? How do you experience Jesus' entry into our condition, our brokenness, our need? How does Jesus' entering into our mess inform God's call to you? In what way is God calling you to enter into the mess of your community to bring healing?

Prayer for the Journey
Come, O Holy Spirit.
Come as Holy Fire and burn in us.
Come as Holy Wind and cleanse us within.
Come as Holy Light and lead us in the darkness.
Come as Holy Truth and dispel our ignorance.
Come as Holy Power and enable our weakness.
Come as Holy Life and dwell in us.
Convict us, convert us, consecrate us,
Until we are set free from the service of ourselves, to be your servants in the world.
Book of Common Worship

THE WILDERNESS JOURNEY

The longest journey is the journey inward.
Dag Hammarskjöld

What follows Jesus' baptism may surprise some. No baptismal cake, no party for the newly baptized. Rather, the Spirit drives Jesus into the wilderness to be tested. Only after being tested will his initiation be complete. Only then will he be prepared for the challenges and rejection that lie ahead.

The wilderness journey is the long journey inward resisted by most, yet the place of God's choosing. Like the Judean desert, the terrain of our souls is often lonely and inhospitable. While we might prefer the speed of highways, this is the path on which our characters are refined, preparing us for a call—not of our own choosing, but of God's heart and will. If we are to become like Jesus, we must share the path he traveled.

Ruth Haley Barton describes the terrain of the wilderness as liminal space. She notes that it:
> "… is a unique spiritual position where human beings hate to be but where the biblical God is always leading them. It is when you have left the tried and true, but have not yet been able to replace it with anything else. It is when you are finally out of the way. It is when you are between your old comfort zone and any possible new answer. If you are not trained in how to hold anxiety, how to live with ambiguity, how to entrust and wait, you will run... anything to flee this terrible cloud of unknowing."

This tenuous, liminal space leads many to look for a quick fix, seeking certainty in any false god that will promise a way out of the desert—even if it means returning to bondage in Egypt. But as anyone who has read the Exodus story knows, there is no going back. Much as we hate "in-between times," they are crucial to unlearning the ways that have enslaved us. It is the only way to live forward into God's new. Jesus has been baptized. The Father's pleasure is made known. The wilderness is the place where Jesus comes to terms with the reality and cost of deep change.

Just as Jesus had to come to terms with the reality that he could not go back to Nazareth and pick up where he left off, so we must also come to terms with the cost of becoming like Jesus. Certain ways of being that once were acceptable are no longer appropriate. Yet we do not have clarity of who we are to become and how we are to be. Letting go must precede taking hold. We must train ourselves to hold anxiety, to live with ambiguity, to entrust and wait. These are just a few lessons born of the wilderness.

Food for the Journey
- Deuteronomy 8:15-16, Israel in the wilderness
- Galatians 5:13-26, Walk by the Spirit
- Mark 1:9-13, Jesus' testing in the wilderness

Journey Questions
1. What role has testing played in shaping you as a disciple?
2. Have you ever been driven by the Spirit into the wilderness?
3. What did the wilderness have to teach you?

Journey Practice: In the Wilderness
Take some time to ponder the two "wilderness" texts below:

> "God led you through that great and terrible wilderness, that thirsty and waterless land, with its venomous snakes and scorpions. He brought you water out of the hard rock. He gave you manna to eat in the wilderness, something your ancestors had never known, to humble and test you so that in the end it might go well with you." Deuteronomy 8:15-16

> "Then Jesus was led by the Spirit into the wilderness to be tempted by the devil." Matthew 4:1

Now enter into a place of stillness with God. Take a few moments to breathe deeply and become aware of God's presence within you and all around you. As you inhale, breathe in the life that God is giving you in this moment. As you exhale, release the distractions that keep you from being fully present to God in this moment.

As you feel ready, reflect on your own journey through the lens of the Israelites' exodus from Egypt and Jesus being driven by the Spirit into the wilderness after his baptism. Where you are on the journey? Go to that place and listen for what God wants to say to you. How is God calling you to hold onto anxiety, to live with ambiguity, to entrust and wait, to dwell in the "not yet"? What is God calling you to learn from the wilderness?

Prayer for the Journey

Spirit of integrity, you drive us into the desert to search out our truth.
Give us clarity to know what is right, and courage to reject what is strategic;
that we may abandon the false innocence of failing to choose at all,
but may follow the purposes of Jesus Christ. Amen.

Janet Morley, *All Desires Known*

CRUCIBLES

When heated directly by fire, the fire of trial,
the heat of disease, Infernos of grief and purity…
Can we hold under the terror, the torment of transforming,
under forging, Until we are bearers of light,
torches, for sufferance, for illumining oblivion.
Susan Deborah King, "Crucible" in <u>One-Breasted Woman</u>

Crucible: a place or occasion of severe test or trial. Try though we might, not one of us can avoid the fire. Each one of us must pass through our own crucible. Each one of us will be changed because of it. For some, it will be a journey born out of illness. For others, the crucible will be shaped by life circumstances. For still others, a poor decision that has far greater impact that could be imagined at the time. Whatever the source, the fire of trial will forever change us. The question is, "can we hold under the terror, the torment of transforming, under forging, until we are bearers of light"?

I believe we resist the wilderness because we know that in it we will encounter our crucible— that place or set of circumstances that subject us to forces that leave us changed, unable to return to the comfort of what we once knew. Crucibles test us to the core of our being. They force us to examine ourselves—our characters and values—and come to grips with who we really are. They are defining moments as we confront the painful tensions within us that a new synthesis of being might take place.

Have you ever wondered about Jesus' petition to God in the Lord's Prayer: "Lead us not into temptation"? I have. I have always wondered if the source of that petition was Jesus' own experience of being led—driven— into the wilderness by the Spirit. He knew the wilderness first-hand. He also knew the frailty of his disciples in the face of temptation. So when asked to teach them to pray, he prays that God would lead them (and us) not into temptation. At the same time, he called them (and us) to take up our cross and follow him (Matthew 16:24).

Knowing our reluctance to experience pain, I sense that the Spirit continues to drive us into the wilderness, providing crucibles by which to stretch and grow us. If we're honest, we know that far too often it takes a crisis before we're willing to deal with our need to change. Those who seek to follow in the Way of Jesus should not be surprised to find that trial and temptation are part of the spiritual journey. All growth entails a certain amount of suffering, pain, and even struggle; all the more so with spiritual growth.

Just as God created us to live in relationship, so God uses trials and temptations to tear down barriers to his love and invitation to life. The gift and the burden of free will means that we must choose between good and evil. Will our actions testify to our core identity in Christ? Will our crucibles become the forge in which our characters are transformed? Can we hold under the terror, the torment of transformation, until we are bearers of light? Or will we choose "safety" over God?

In the end, whom will we serve?

Food for the Journey
- Zechariah 13:1-9, Cleaning from sin
- Acts 5:25-42, We must obey God
- Matthew 2:1-17, Jesus being tempted in the wilderness

Journey Questions
1. Why do you think Jesus includes "lead us not into temptation" as a petition in the Lord's Prayer? Of what are you tempted?
2. What has been your experience of the Refiner's fire?
3. How have your crucible(s) forged your character in Christ?

Journey Practice: Write a Letter
Poet May Sarton writes of her journey: "Now I become myself. It's taken time, many years and places, / I have been dissolved and shaken. Worn other people's faces…"

The wilderness is often the means by which we become ourselves and come home to our true selves. It is the place where we are laid bare, where our crucibles allow us to look realistically and honestly at ourselves without denial, indulgence or embellishment. Though painful, our crucibles afford us the opportunity to come to terms with unresolved anger, disappointments, losses, and fears. As we do so, the fire burns away all that is not true, while also nurturing compassion and hope. Some aspects of the journey must be lived before they can be fully understood. Even so, we can share from those defining moments the ways in which we have been changed and blessed.

This next week, write a letter to God (or yourself, or your child(ren), or someone you are mentoring). Describe your journey through the wilderness. Tell of how ways that it has refined you and made you who you are today. How did your crucible help you discover your essential self, your core identity in Christ?

What did you need to release in order to become who you are? In what ways was your character refined?

Prayer for the Journey

Purify my heart. Let me be as gold and precious silver.
Purify my heart. Let me be as gold, pure gold.
Refiner's fire, My heart's one desire Is to be holy.
Set apart for You, Lord. I choose to be holy.
Set apart for You, my Master, Ready to do Your will.
Purify my heart, Cleanse me from within And make me holy.
Purify my heart. Cleanse me from my sin, Deep within.
Brian Doerksen

SHADOW BOXING

There is no light without shadow and no psychic wholeness without imperfection. To round itself out life...calls not for perfection but for completeness and for this the 'thorn in the flesh' is needed, the suffering of defects without which there is no progress and no ascent.
C.G. Jung

When Arthur Ramsey was Archbishop of Canterbury, he would frequently remind disciples that the whole Jesus demands the whole person. A good reminder for all who seek to follow Jesus! The challenge is that bringing the whole person before Jesus involves acknowledging our shadow sides, something we shy away from at a great cost, not only to ourselves, but also to those with whom we live and work.

In large part, I think that shame holds us back: the shame of being less than perfect. In a culture where mistakes are not allowed, we tend to deny and even hide our shadow sides. After all, hiding from God has been modeled to us since the beginning with Adam and Eve in the Fall. But as Jung reminds us: "There is no light without shadow and no psychic wholeness without imperfection."

Most of us from early on are trained to share only our "good" sides, those parts of ourselves that make us and others look good. In many instances, we are rewarded not only for hiding our shadow sides, but even sometimes for nurturing them. Of course, the cost is great. Bit by bit, our souls shrivel and die within us. In Jesus' words, we become hypocrites (literally, in the Greek, "actors") who deny our very humanity. We become people who play roles, rather than live lives.

Not only is there a place, but a need, for healthy shame. Not one of us will make it through this life without making mistakes and even failing. Healthy shame lets us know that we are human and keeps us grounded in Christ. As John Bradshaw writes in *Healing the Shame that Binds You*: "Healthy shame [...] is the emotional energy that signals us that we are not God, that we will make mistakes, that we need help. Healthy shame gives us permission to be human."

A key means by which we come to experience and grow from healthy shame is through what Richard Rohr calls "shadow boxing." Shadow boxing involves bringing the messiness, the pain and brokenness of our lives into the light. It involves examination of motives and confession. It involves exposure. For only as we bring our whole selves before Jesus can we walk in the light without fear of exposure.

To be sure, there will be moments of humiliation. But humiliation is the means by which we come to practice *kenosis*, the emptying of self that we might be filled with the glory of God. Shadow boxing becomes the means by which we come to know what it means to be fearfully and wonderfully made in the image of God.

Are you ready to do some shadow boxing?

Food for the Journey
- Genesis 1, Created in the image of God
- Romans 12:1-3, Transformed by the renewing of our minds
- Luke 4:1-13, Jesus is tested in the wilderness

Journey Questions
1. What does it mean to be created in the image of God?
2. How are we to be transformed by the renewing of our minds?
3. What insights does Luke's account of Jesus' temptation offer?

Journey Practice: "Shadow Boxing"
"Shadow boxing" allows us to bring that which is hidden into the light. Sometimes it drives us to name repressed anger. Other times it leads to acknowledging sadness within us, thereby it opens us up to healing, reveals our vulnerabilities, and even helps us to connect more fully with others. Still other times we encounter a fear which, when named, we are able to detach from and look at more objectively. Shadow boxing can open us up to deep joy as we discover previously untapped creativity and energy. This joy becomes the means to become more of the person God created us to be. Our encounter with our shadows plays a central role in the process of being transformed by the renewing of our minds (Romans 12:1-3). Parker Palmer in *Let Your Life Speak* names five shadows that we would do well to own:

1. Insecurity about Identity and Worth: When we forget who and whose we are, we seek to prove our worth through activity. The counterpoint to this unceasing activity is to heed the call to "be still and know that God is God" (Psalm 46:10).
2. Belief that the universe is a battleground: Yet scripture tells us that God works through all things for the good for those who love him

(Romans 8:28). This reality behooves us to ponder the reality of God's original intent for creation. To be sure, we live in a competitive world, but how much of that is our creation?

3. <u>Functional atheism</u>: This is the belief that the outcome depends upon us. According to Palmer, such convictions lead to pathology on all levels, eventually causing burnout and stress on relationships to the breaking point. For this reason (among others), Jesus calls us to learn "the unforced rhythms of grace" (Matthew 11:28-30, *The Message*).

4. <u>Fear (especially of the natural chaos of life)</u>: Yet chaos is a precondition to creativity. God created out of chaos. Messiness comes with innovation and change.

5. <u>Denial of death</u>: It is helpful to remember the wisdom of Chaucer: There is an end to everything, to good things as well (c. 1374). When we fail to allow things a natural death, we find ourselves unable to live forward. But when we claim the reality that death precedes resurrection and we allow death, we are set free to live into God's new.

Prayer for the Journey
O Eternal One, it would be easier for me to pray if I were clear and of a single mind and pure heart, if I could be done hiding from myself and from you, even in my prayers. But I am who I am, mixture of motives and excuses, blur of memories, quiver of hopes, knot of fear, tangle of confusion, and restless with love for love... Come, find me, Lord. Be with me exactly as I am. Help me find me, Lord. Help me accept what I am so I can begin to be yours.
Ted Loder, <u>Guerillas of Grace</u>

SIN HAPPENS!

Sin happens whenever we refuse to keep growing.
Gregory of Nyssa

Now there is a new take on "S&!% Happens!" I wonder how folks would respond to a rewriting of the Anglo-Saxon version of that bumper sticker. Not only would it clean up the language, it would also challenge us to put "sin" in perspective.

In a culture that is over-sensitized to sin (at least the sins of others), it would call us to reflect on sin from a new angle. (Please note that I am *not* encouraging us all to go out and sin that grace may abound!) I am suggesting that we take a look at our own contradictions and foibles from the perspective of formation: our growing up in Christ, rather than do's and don'ts. We could use some generosity of spirit when responding to both our own sins and those of others.

As Richard Rohr reminds us in *Falling Upward*, "Sin and salvation are correlative terms. Salvation is not sin perfectly avoided, as the ego would prefer; but in fact, salvation is sin turned on its head and used in our favor." It is helpful to note that even virtues overused can become sin. (Really!)

As noted:
- Honesty in the absence of compassion becomes cruelty.
- Tenacity unmediated by flexibility congeals into rigidity.
- Confidence untempered by humility is arrogance.
- Courage without prudence is recklessness.

The ancients call this honoring of seemingly paradoxical virtues *anacoluthia*, or "the mutual entailment of virtues." Put simply, no virtue is a virtue by itself.

Rohr continues, "I do not think you should get rid of your sin until you have learned what it has to teach you. Otherwise, it will only return in new forms, as Jesus says of the 'unclean spirit' that returns to the house all 'swept and tidied' (Luke 11:24-26); then he rightly and courageously says that 'the last state of the house will be worse than the first.'"

We live in a world that increasingly thinks in "either/or" terms. In our desire to reflect favored virtues, we fail to understand that the favored

79

virtues of others have the potential to stretch and grow us ever more fully into the image of God. Sin happens, Gregory of Nyssa reminds us, whenever we refuse to keep growing.

Food for the Journey
- Psalm 51, Create in me a clean heart
- Romans 7:7-25, The Law and sin
- Luke 11:24-26, Unclean spirits

Journey Questions
1. When you think of "sin," what comes to mind?
2. How does the early church father's belief that "sin happens whenever we refuse to keep growing" reframe your understanding of sin?
3. What have you learned from your sins? How have those learnings nurtured compassion for others in their brokenness?

Journey Practice: Pondering Sin
The temptation of Jesus brings home the demands of the formational journey. This week, take some time to prayerfully ponder the unclean spirits found in Luke 11. Why, upon sweeping one out, did seven return? What does this have to tell us about the difference between behavior modification and character transformation? The Adversary uses predictable ways to get at us: through our hunger, our need for security, our desire for power.

Each of us has particular weaknesses that leave us open to temptation. In what areas are you most vulnerable? What family-of-origin issues influence how you deal with temptation? What are your memories of early temptations? How did you deal with them? In light of Jesus' model in the wilderness, what would you do differently?

After reflecting on the challenge of temptation, ponder Gregory of Nyssa's challenge that sin happens whenever we refuse to keep growing. How is God calling you to grow that you might more fully embody Christ in your life? Never forget that "incarnation is a difficult lesson for anyone to learn."

Prayer for the Journey

Take, Lord, all my liberty, my memory, my understanding, and my whole will.
You have given me all that I have, all that I am,
and I surrender all to your Divine will.
Give me only Your love and Your grace.
With this I am rich enough, and I have no more to ask.
Ignatius of Loyola

GOD POWER AND *KENOSIS*

God has given us the power to change our ways.
God has given us the power to change our ways.
Feed the hungry, loose the bound. Walk humbly with our God.
Mechtild of Magdeburg

Entering the mess. The wilderness. Crucibles. Shadow boxing. All are means by which God seeks to empty us. *Kenosis* ("the emptying of self") is at the heart of Jesus' incarnation and God's call to us as to feed the hungry, lose the bound, and walk humbly. The wilderness is ultimately a place of emptying, not for the sake of personal salvation, but that we might embrace holiness for the sake of the world.

Only transformed disciples can bear transformation. Most of us shy away from the practice of *kenosis* because, intuitively, we know the cost. But it is the only way. We come to learn God's power is not like human power. John the Baptist is clear: we must decrease that Christ might increase within us. In the words of Paul, "our attitude should be the same as Christ Jesus: who, being by very nature God, did not consider equality with God as something to be grasped, but made himself nothing, taking the very nature of a servant, being made in human likeness. And being found in appearance as a man, he humbled (he emptied himself) and became obedient unto death—even death on a cross" (Philippians 2:5-8).

While a part of the wilderness journey is predicated upon the need to change born of our sin and brokenness, that is only part of the journey. We must also be emptied even of "the good" that holds us apart from God. *Kenosis* becomes the means by which Christ-like character is forged in and through humility. This part of the journey involves surrendering control and leaves us forever changed.

The surrendered life is about God power. We can use power to afflict or set free: the choice remains ours. Much of how we use power depends upon how well we have journeyed through the wilderness. In Jesus, God models a power that is both self-giving and self-limiting. *Kenosis* leads us beyond a focus on personal survival to an emptying that becomes the means by which the kingdom of God enters this world, without regard to cost to self. Our integrity as disciples will be measured by the degree to which we too bear the kingdom into the lives of others. As the apostle Paul reminds us, "The reign of God is not just words, it is power" (I Corinthians 4:20).

Of what is God calling you to empty yourself of that you might seek and bear the kingdom of God into the world? Take some time this next week to ponder this question—with God and with trusted friends. Dare to surrender yourself to God in prayer that God might use you. Never forget that emptying is prelude to filling!

Food for the Journey
- Micah 6:6-8, Walk humbly
- Philippians 2:1-11, Emptied
- John 3:22-36, I must decrease

Journey Questions
1. Of what do you need to empty yourself in order to live a fully surrendered life? Is it renunciation of your own agenda? Detachment from a certain way of being? Letting go of expectations of a particular outcome?
2. Take some time to ponder your attachments. Ask yourself, in what way is God calling you to be emptied that you might following in the way of Jesus?

Journey Practice: Emptied!
If Jesus is our model for our life's journey, then we need to take seriously his response to both the brokenness of others on the riverbank and his wilderness experience. Take some time this week to reread the gospel accounts of his baptism and testing in the wilderness. Note the images that come to you. Select one that is particularly striking for you and meditate on that image, letting it become concrete. As you do this, ponder the questions below:
- What does this image of Jesus say to you about power?
- What does this image say to you about self-awareness and self-management?
- What does this image say about God's call?

Prayer for the Journey
Gracious and Holy One, Creator of all things and of emptiness,
I come to you full of much that clutters and distracts, stifles and burdens me,
and makes me a burden to others.
Empty me now of growing dissatisfactions, of anxious imaginings,
of fretful preoccupations, of nagging prejudices, of old scores to settle,
and of the arrogance of being right.

Empty me of the ways I unthinkingly think of myself as powerless,
as a victim, determined by sex, age, race, as being less than I am,
of as other than yours.
Empty me of the disguises and lies in which I hide myself from other people
and from my responsibility for my neighbors and for the world.
Hollow out in me a space, in which I will find myself,
find peace and a whole heart, a forgiving spirit and holiness, the springs of laughter,
and the will to reach boldly for abundant life for myself and the whole human family.
Ted Loder, <u>Guerillas of Grace</u>

AND THE ANGELS MINISTERED

Then the devil left him, and behold,
angels came and were ministering to him.
Matthew 4:11

Can you allow others to care for you when you are in need? I do not mean paid services. I mean, can you receive care from God's messengers (be they angelic or human) when you are exhausted and depleted?

To spend forty days and nights in the wilderness fasting is more than draining. To then be tempted by the Adversary had to have drained every last vestige of strength from Jesus, leaving him victorious but utterly depleted. It is then that God sends angels to minister unto him.

Many of us have been raised to pull ourselves up by our own bootstraps. But this is not on what Jesus models in his earthly life. Time and again, our incarnate Lord allows others to care for him: Martha, Mary, Lazarus, the disciples, Peter's mother-in-law (after being healed by Jesus), the woman who washed his feet with her hair, and even the Samaritan woman at the well. Jesus receives care from others. He is not afraid to name his needs.

Throughout his ministry, he balances times of stress with times of renewal. Time together in community is followed by time apart with the Father. Acts of giving are balanced with acts of receiving. Jesus knew what we are only now coming to name: stress must be balanced by recovery, or we will not be able to sustain ourselves for the journey. As Loehr and Schwartz write in *The Power of Full Engagement*, "Any form of stress that prompts discomfort has the potential to expand our capacity—physically, mentally, emotionally or spiritually—so long as it is followed by adequate recovery."

Stress and renewal: We need both if we are to become like Jesus. We must be attentive to the need to not only care for self, but also receive care from others. God chose to enter this world as an infant, dependent upon the care of earthly parents. Even as an adult, Jesus remained dependent upon the care of others. Why then are we, who are human, so resistant to receiving care from others?

Food for the Journey
- Genesis 28:10-22, Jacob's ladder
- I Peter 3:8-9, Be compassionate
- Matthew 4:11, The devil left and the angels came and ministered

Journey Questions
1. If an audit were to be done of your life—physical, emotional, mental, and spiritual aspects—would it reflect a balance between stress and renewal?
2. Are you able to receive from others? Why or why not?
3. What is your understanding of care? What particular experiences have shaped your ability (or inability) to receive from others?

Journey Practice: Stress and Renewal

Jesus modeled with his life a balance between being and doing. He did not expect the disciples to immediately understand their need for both stress and renewal; Rather, he taught them through word and action how to live. He embodied a way of being that incorporated both giving of self and receiving from others. In systems language, he neither over-functioned, nor under-functioned. (By contrast, we tend toward one extreme or the other. Often, birth order and expectations of our families of origin play a role in which extreme we take.)

During this week, draw up a list of the ways you give to others and another list of those from whom you receive care. Next to the list of those for whom you care, write down the ways in which you care for them. Next to the list of those who care for you, write down the ways that you receive care. What do these two lists tell you about the balance of giving and receiving in your life? If you asked three people close to you to honestly name your tendency to either over- or under- function, what would they tell you? Are you at risk for burn-out? Or are you failing to stretch yourself to your full potential? How does your life evidence a balance between stress and renewal? Outline a care plan in which you seek to balance care of self with care for others.

Prayer for the Journey

We give you thanks, Gentle One who has touched our soul.
You have loved us from the moment of our first awakening and have held us in joy and in grief. Stay with us we pray. Grace us with your presence and with it the fullness of our own humanity. Help us claim our strength and need, our awesomeness and fragile beauty, that encouraged by the truth we might work to restore compassion to the human family.
Janet Schaffran and Pat Kozak, <u>More than Words</u>

The Journey:
Growing Up in Christ

Engagement

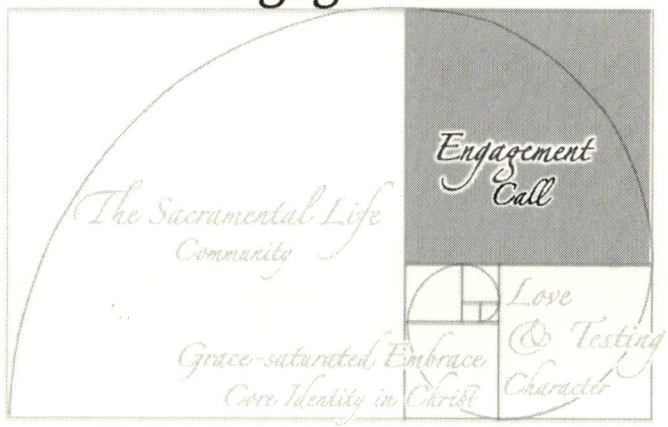

ENGAGEMENT

The Spirit of the Lord is upon me because he has anointed me to proclaim good news to the poor. He has sent me to proclaim freedom for the prisoners and recovery of sight to the blind, to set the oppressed free, to proclaim the year of the Lord's favor.
Luke 4:18-19

Having been prepared, first through the grace-saturated embrace and then through love and testing, the time comes to engage with the world through the living of God's call. Each one of us is gifted with strengths and passions by which we are to bless the world. Marjorie Zoet Bankson in *The Call of Soul* describes God's call as "an invitation to wholeness, a spiritual prompting to complete the work of love that we are here to do."

We can never be whole apart from heeding God's call. Only as we engage with the world that God loved so much to send his only Son will we come to experience the wholeness of Shalom. As the prophet Jeremiah reminds us, we each are called to "seek the Shalom of the communities to which we have been sent in exile; for in their Shalom will be our Shalom" (29:7).

In his ministry, Jesus models for us how we are to engage with the world: He invites us to experience the reign of God through his preaching, teaching and healing. He models a life given to God and lived for God's mission.

The Spirit of God is upon us, for God has anointed us to proclaim the good news through our engagement with the world!

A MESSAGE TO PROCLAIM

Jesus became who we are that we might become what he is.
Irenaeus

Soon after his testing in the wilderness, Jesus preached in his home synagogue: "The Spirit of the Lord is upon me because he has anointed me to proclaim good news to the poor. He has sent me to proclaim freedom for the prisoners and recovery of sight to the blind, to set the oppressed free, to proclaim the year of the Lord's favor" (Luke 4:18-19).

At the heart of these words is the call to extend the radical hospitality of God. Jesus both taught and modeled with his life that it is in the space between the stranger and the self that the divine is encountered.

As he told his disciples: "When I was thirsty, you gave me water [...] as you did to the least of these..." (Matthew 25:45). Quoting the prophet Isaiah, Jesus proclaims the radical hospitality of God, which beckons all the excluded, disabled and powerless with the promise of healing and wholeness: *Shalom.*

At first the words seem to welcome Jesus' neighbors, and the synagogue warms with pleasure. But, with sickening rapidity, it grows cold as Jesus makes clear that he knows that they do not really understand or truly welcome him. In no time at all, the congregation turns into a lynch mob and Jesus narrowly escapes with his life.

Henri Nouwen talks about the challenges of practicing radical hospitality born of the acceptable time of the Lord: "Hospitality means primarily the creation of free space where the stranger can enter and become a friend instead of an enemy. Hospitality is not to change people, but to offer them space where change can take place. It is not to bring men and women over to our side, but to offer freedom not disturbed by dividing lines."

Our unity, then, is found in Christ. But there is danger here: there will be change. Part of the spiritual practice of radical hospitality is to learn to recognize our internal reactions to people whom we consider "strangers." It is to name our fear of change and make a conscious decision to "let go." To whom do we find it hardest to extend hospitality? What of our past will be the hardest to "let go" of that there might be space for "the new" born of God's call? The answers for each of us are probably different. Yet, we do well to remember that Jesus became who we are that we might become what he is.

Radical hospitality is more than welcoming the stranger in our midst. It is an ongoing spiritual practice that challenges each one of us to look beneath superficial differences to engage the holiness that is the foundation of every person. Like every spiritual practice, it is meant to change us until we come to bear the image of Christ.

Food for the Journey
- Isaiah 61, The Year of the Lord's favor
- Acts 2:14-41, Peter's first sermon
- Luke 4:14-30, Jesus is rejected at Nazareth

Journey Questions
1. How is God calling you to "proclaim the year of the Lord's favor"?
2. To whom do you find it hardest to extend hospitality?
3. How is hospitality understood in the church today? How does this differ from the biblical accounts? Reflect on the significance of these differences.
4. Who are the strangers or enemies in our lives today? What would offering them hospitality look like? What would make it possible to do so?

Journey Practice: Hospitality
"I was a stranger and you invited me in." Jesus, Matthew 25:35b.

How is God calling you to practice radical hospitality? Often, hospitality is understood to be synonymous with "friendliness." While not mutually exclusive, hospitality calls us to a deeper investment of self than simple friendliness demands. Hospitality calls us to share our stories, with both laughter and tears. Hospitality pulls us into a deeper relationship with God and one another. Jesus makes clear that offering hospitality is a moral imperative (Matthew 25), and that our fears do not excuse us from welcoming the stranger in our midst. It is interesting to note that the word for "stranger" in Greek (*xenos*) also means "guest" and "host." In fact, the New Testament word for "hospitality" (*philoxenia*) literally translates as "a love of guests or strangers." How might our lives change if we dared to greet each person we meet as Christ in the stranger's guise?

Prayer for the Journey

Fearful God, you require of our love appalling sacrifice;
and your lasting promise is contained in contradiction.
May we so lay on your altar our dearest desires
that we may receive them back from you as unaccountable gift,
through Jesus Christ. Amen.
Janet Morley, <u>All Desires Known</u>

THE CALLING OF THE TWELVE

*God has created me to do Him some definite service; He has committed
some work to me which He has not committed to another... I have a
part in a great work; I am a link in a chain, a bond of connection
between persons. He has not created me for naught.
I shall love as Christ loved, I shall be his work.*
John Henry Newman

"Jesus went up on a mountainside and called to him those he wanted, and
they came to him. He appointed twelve—designating them apostles—that
they might be with him and that he might send them out ..." (Mark 3:13-
15). From the beginning, Jesus has modeled that together we are the body
of Christ and individually members of that body (I Corinthians 12). Unlike
the rabbis of his day, he did not seat himself in the synagogue and wait for
disciples to come and sit with him. Rather, he prayed to God and called
those whom God appointed: "Come, follow me." And follow they did.

Having called them, he then trained them. First, he showed them how to do
the ministries to which they were called—preaching, teaching and healing.
Then he sent them out two by two to engage in works of ministry. He also
modeled for them the balance needed between time together and time
apart. He knew that they would struggle to learn that he is the source and
that they must abide in him if they want to do the work to which he calls us
(John 15). The same teachings remain true for us.

Like Moses, all too often we take on burdens God never intended for us to
carry alone. Like Moses, we find ourselves burned out and over-extended.
And, it takes those who are like Jethro in our lives to tell us that "this is not
good," and the work is meant to be shared and delegated among many.
The Apostle Paul makes clear it that we are to serve out of our gifts. God
has created each one of us for a purpose. Part of the joy and challenge is to
discern that purpose. It begins with coming to know ourselves in Christ as
we claim the reality that each one of us is called through our baptism.

Business consultant Peter Drucker once said that most people think they
know their gifts, and most are wrong. Odd, yet I believe this is because
many of us carry the burden of expectations placed on our shoulders by
others (often unintentionally). By contrast, Jesus calls us to place "his yoke"
on our shoulders that we might learn "the unforced rhythms of grace"
(Matthew 11:28-30, *The Message*).

Gifts. Passions. Needs. All play a role in discerning and living out God's call. As Paul reminds us: "God is our Maker and in our union with Christ, God has created us for a life of good works which has already been prepared for us to do" (see Ephesians 2:10). The challenge is to discern that for which we have been created. Therein lies our greatest joy as we become the people we were created to be by God. It is then we are set free to serve with energy, intelligence, imagination, and love. It is then that we most fully engage with our world in the name of Jesus.

Food for the Journey
- Exodus 18:13-27, Jethro advises Moses to delegate responsibility
- Romans 12:1-8, The body of Christ
- Mark 3:13-15, The calling of the twelve

Journey Questions
1. What do these three texts have to teach us about call?
2. Who is your "Jethro"? Are you currently engaged in a ministry that leaves you feeling over-extended and on the brink of burn-out? What is God seeking to tell you through your "Jethro"?
3. How has God called you to serve? Do you know your gifts? Would others agree with you?
4. Do you know "the good works" that God has prepared for you to do?
5. When have you felt most alive in your service? When have you found yourself set free to serve with energy, intelligence, imagination and love?

Journey Practice: Heeding God's Call
This week, take some time apart to ponder God's call to you. Pray through the words of John Bell's hymn "The Summons," allowing them to become for you a means of recommitting yourself to God's call anew.

Will you come and follow me If I but call your name?
Will you go where you don't know And never be the same?
Will you let my love be shown, Will you let my name be known,
Will you let my life be grown In you and you in me?
　　Will you leave yourself behind If I but call your name?
　　Will you care for cruel and kind And never be the same?
　　Will you risk the hostile stare Should your life attract or scare?
　　Will you let me answer pray'r In you and you in me?
Will you let the blinded see If I but call your name?
Will you set the prisoners free And never be the same?

Will you kiss the leper clean, And do such as this unseen,
And admit to what I mean In you and you in me?

> *Will you love the 'you' you hide If I but call your name?*
> *Will you quell the fear inside And never be the same?*
> *Will you use the faith you've found To reshape the world around,*
> *Through my sight and touch and sound In you and you in me?*

Lord, your summons echoes true When you but call my name.
Let me turn and follow you And never be the same.
In your company I'll go Where your love and footsteps show.
Thus I'll move and live and grow In you and you in me.
John Bell, The Iona Community

Prayer for the Journey
Look at your hands, see and touch the tenderness—God's own for the world.
Look at your feet, see the path and the direction—God's own for the world.
Look at your heart, see the fire and the love—God's own for the world.
Look at the cross, see God's Son and our Savior—God's own for the world.
This is God's world and we will serve God in it.
Wild Goose Worship Group, <u>A Wee Worship Book</u>, 1989

TEACHING IN PARABLES

Jesus spoke all these things to the crowd in parables;
he did not say anything to them without using a parable.
Matthew 13:34

"The kingdom of God is like:
... a grain of mustard seed which a man took and sowed in the field; it
is the smallest of seed but when it is grown it is the greatest of shrubs.
... leaven which a woman took and hid in three measures of flour, till
it all was leavened.
... a merchant in search of fine pearls, who, upon finding one pearl of
great value, went and sold all that he had and bought it."

Again and again, Jesus uses parables to invite his listeners (and us) into a
new way of being. He who came to proclaim the reign of God did so not
only through his healing and casting out of demons, but also through his
teaching and preaching. His metaphors for God's reign are often both
simple, yet unexpected: a grain of mustard, leaven, a fine pearl. Even as he
uses simple, everyday images, there is a sense of mystery.

Every time we think we have understood what the reign of God is like, we
find ourselves confronted with another (sometimes conflicting) image. For
the kingdom is both present and future. It touches us as individuals, while
also calling us to community. It addresses not only the spiritual, but the
physical life. Ultimately, participation in the kingdom requires participation
in the life, death, and resurrection of Jesus.

While signs of the kingdom can (sometimes) be found in the church, often
it is encountered far from organized religion. The vision shared through
story and parable was (and is) an assault on the social and economic
structures shaped by humanity. Jesus knew the power of parable—of
metaphor—to disorient and thereby reorient. As so, through his parables,
Jesus sets before us two ways of being: one, the ordinary and the other, the
extraordinary.

Few of us like to be told anything, save the good that we have done.
Perhaps that is why Jesus chose to speak in parables. Rather than telling, he
invited us to ponder. Taking common images, he uses paradox to challenge
and invite us into a different way of being.

Ultimately, Jesus' very life serves as a parable. New Testament scholar Leander Keck describes the earthly life of Jesus as "a parabolic event of the kingdom of God." He who spoke in parables was himself a parable who shocked and disturbed, upset conventions and expectations, and thereby invited humanity into a different way of being that had (and has) revolutionary potential. His earthly journey provides coordinates for our earthly journey as both pilgrim and steward. It is not uncommon to find that people who disdain the church are deeply attracted to the person of Jesus. Nevertheless, there is an audacious quality to admitting that we seek to become like Jesus. Herein lies both challenge and call.

"The kingdom of God is like…" Knowing Jesus, shaped by the Word, how are we to answer that question? How are we to live God's reign?

Food for the Journey
- Isaiah 11:1-9, The peaceable kingdom
- I Corinthians 15:50-58, The Resurrection
- Matthew 13:34-35, Speaking in parables

Journey Questions
1. What is your experience of the reign of God? Do you perceive it as a future hope or a reality already present, at least in part?
2. How does the prophetic image of the peaceable kingdom inform our understanding of the reign of God?
3. What does it mean to live as "people of the resurrection"?
4. How have Jesus' parables informed you in your faith and witness? What parables most challenge your understanding of "kingdom living"?

Journey Practice: Become a Parabolic Event
"The limits of our language are the limits of our world" (Ludwig Wittgenstein).

In a time of dogmatic literalism, Wittgenstein's wisdom calls us to remember the power and importance of language to either limit or expand our world. As you reflect on your present journey, pick several metaphors from scripture to ponder God's call to you. Is there a particular song, animal, plant, or book of the Bible that provides metaphorical insight? Take time to not only ponder, but journal your responses to three to four images. Then choose one of Jesus' parables to pray through. Reflect on the images from scripture as they inform your response to the parable. How is God calling you to be "a parabolic event of the reign of God"?

Prayer for the Journey

Almighty God, Father of our Lord Jesus Christ,
grant, we pray, that we might be grounded and settled
in your truth by the coming of the Holy Spirit into our hearts.
What we do not know, reveal to us;
What is lacking within us, make complete;
That which we do know, confirm in us;
And keep us blameless in your service;
Through Jesus Christ our Lord. Amen.
Clement of Rome

HEALING

Do you want to be healed?
Jesus (John 5:6)

"Do you want to be healed?" Again and again, Jesus asks this question of those who seek his help. One of the things that Jesus demanded of those he encountered in his ministry is that they name their wounds. Be it the return of sight or hearing, the ability to walk again, the healing of a relationship, whatever the need, Jesus insisted that those who came to him be specific— not for his sake, but for theirs.

It sounds obvious, but naming our need for healing is often more difficult than we realize. As we know from several medical studies, what people believe to be feeling the need of hunger is often dehydration. We are so out of touch with our body that we are unable to differentiate between the need for food and the need for drink. No wonder we have such a difficult time naming our deeper wounds and needs!

We spend our lives climbing the proverbial corporate ladder, even devoting ourselves to good works, until one day we wake up and think, "For what?" We hurt. We know ourselves to be empty, but we can't name the source of the pain. For some, the yearning is so deep, the dislocation so intense, that it becomes difficult to think of life without the pain.

"Do you want to be healed?" Jesus asks us. The inherent promise, of course, is that when we say yes to Jesus' question ("Yes, we want to be healed. Yes, we want to be whole. Yes, we want to be filled with Jesus."), then the path to wholeness is opened. This is God's promise.

To be sure, wholeness does not always mean cure. Paul carried "the thorn in his side" until the day he died. But we have something better than even a cure. We have wholeness.

Food for the Journey
- Psalm 30, The Lord healed me
- James 5:14-16, Laying on of hands
- John 5, Healing of the sick man by the pool of Bethesda

Journey Questions
1. How do you respond to Jesus' question: Do you want to be healed?
2. Are you able to name the source of your wounds? For what do you hunger and thirst?
3. Are you open to receiving the laying on of hands and prayers of the elders?

Journey Practice: Attend a Healing Service
The New Testament describes how Jesus and the early church not only prayed for the sick, but also laid hands on them. Touching, anointing, praying: three simple acts that both comfort and convey the healing power of God at work. In a high-tech time, we need "high touch." We also need to attend to our whole person: body, mind, emotions and spirit. Over the next several weeks, explore the possibility of attending a healing service in a local congregation or at a nearby retreat center. Don't wait for a doctor's diagnosis to receive prayer and laying on of hands for healing and wholeness.

Prayer for the Journey
O God, gather me to be with you and you are with me.
Keep me in touch with myself,
with my needs, my anxieties, my angers, my pains, my corruptions,
that I may claim them as my own rather than blame them on someone else.
O Lord, deepen my wounds into wisdom; shape my weakness into compassion; gentle my
envy into enjoyment; my fear into trust; my guilt into honesty.
O God, gather me to be with you as you are with me.
Ted Loder, <u>Guerillas of Grace</u>

FEEDING

The ground of compassion is love and the working of compassion keeps us in love. Compassion is a sweet gracious working in love, mingled with abundant kindness.
Julian of Norwich, <u>Revelation of Divine Love</u>

News of Jesus' ministry was spreading. He had healed people of their diseases and his popularity was becoming enormous. But it was also tragedy time in Israel. According to the Gospel of Matthew, John the Baptist had just been beheaded. John the Baptist had been the greatest moral force, the greatest spiritual force, the greatest prophet that the land of Israel had experienced for four hundred years. He was the person that everyone looked to for religious inspiration—and he was just beheaded by King Herod.

Everyone was stunned by this tragedy and enormous loss, including Jesus, who had been baptized by John. And so it was grieving time in Israel. Mourning time. Jesus wanted to get away by himself to grieve, to pray, to remember. He got into a boat to sail across Lake Galilee, to a remote point some four miles away, in order to get away from the massive crowds who were following him, to be alone and grieve the loss of John the Baptist. But the crowds followed along the shoreline, keeping an eye on his boat, and so when Jesus' boat landed, many of the crowd had already arrived.

What was his reaction to the thousands who had shown up? Irritated? Angry? Imposed upon? No. He looked on the massive crowd with compassion. Like they were sheep without a shepherd, these were people who were in need of spiritual feeding for their inner spiritual hungers. And so Jesus taught them and he healed them. The day quickly passed, and one of the disciples said: "Lord, the hour is late and the people don't have any food. We are a long way from any villages. Maybe you should send them home now."

And Jesus said to Philip (according to John's version of the story), "How are we going to buy bread, so that people can eat?" Jesus said this *in order to test* Philip. Philip replied, "It would take more than two hundred denarii, more than two hundred days of wages, and even that wouldn't be enough bread to feed all these people." Jesus said, "Look around the crowd and see what you can find."

Andrew found a young boy with five loaves of bread and two fish, and brought the boy, fish and bread to Jesus. Jesus invited everyone to be seated on the grass. Jesus took the bread and gazed into heaven. He gave thanks and broke it, and gave it to his disciples, who gave it to the crowds. And they all ate and were all satisfied, *and* there were twelve baskets of bread left over. The number who ate were five thousand men, plus women and children.

That story was told over and over again in the gospels, but it continued. A few days later, Jesus was out in the wilderness with a large crowd (four thousand men plus women and children), and the same story happens *again!* This time, seven loaves and a few fish were found. And once again, Jesus took the bread and looked up into heaven. He gave thanks, broke it and gave it to his disciples, who shared it with the crowd. Everyone ate and was satisfied, and this time there were seven baskets of bread left over. When we read the version of this story in the Gospel of John, we discover that the feeding of the five thousand is prelude to Jesus' teaching that "I am the Bread of life."

Jesus can work miracles with five loaves and two fish. God will do the same with us when we bring our meager gifts to God of five loaves and two fish: our ordinary talents and gifts.

Food for the Journey
- Zechariah 7:8-10, Show compassion
- Galatians 4:8-20 (focus v. 19), Labor until Christ is formed in you
- John 6 and Matthew 9:35-37, Jesus had compassion

Journey Questions
1. Implied in the story is this question: Have you surrendered your five loaves and two fish to Christ? Have you surrendered the meagerness of who you are to Christ? Why or why not?
2. How does Jesus' feeding of the five thousand help us to understand communion?
3. Jesus was grieving his cousin's death, yet he had compassion on the crowd. Can you think of a time when you were in deep personal need, yet God called you first to have compassion on others before caring for yourself?

Journey Practice: Communion

Poet Gunilla Norris writes that "we are united through sharing[, ...] our lives made meaningful [... and] made new. 'Take. Eat. This is my body,' said Jesus when he broke the bread at the Last Supper. Then he gave his life for us. Behind all communion is the knowledge that we must give our lives to each other, for each other."

How is God calling you in this next week to give your life to and for your community? How will you honor that call?

Prayer for the Journey

O God, you have so greatly loved us, long sought us, and mercifully redeemed us.
Give us grace that in everything we may yield ourselves, our wills and our works,
a continual thank-offering to you: through Jesus Christ our Lord.
Amen.

BEFORE DAWN: TIME WITH THE FATHER

A certain unavailability is essential for the spiritual life.
Henri Nouwen

Jesus understood the importance of time alone with the Father. Even if it meant getting up early before dawn, he sought out time with the Father. It didn't matter that the day before was long and hard. Indeed, the intensity of the day underscored his need for time apart. He knew that the Father was his life source and that without Him, he could do nothing.

The same is true of us. As Jesus was to later tell the disciples, "Abide in me and I in you, for apart from me you can do nothing" (John 15:4). Communion with God is a prerequisite to kingdom service. It is the place (or rather, state of being) that opens us up to the movement of the Spirit in our midst. Communion is a spiritual state that we often resist (for reasons we can't even articulate), yet it is the state we yearn for. And when we enter that state, we know ourselves to be blessed as we simply rest in God.

Without communion there can be no compassion for others, nor do we truly intercede for those entrusted to our care. We are too preoccupied with ourselves. Jesus' capacity to be with God deepened his ability to be with us in all our fractured brokenness. In his time apart, he was often present to God on our behalf, listening. It is that same listening that we are called to today that the Spirit might intercede with sighs too deep for words (Romans 8:26-27).

Not that we understand this much better than the disciples. When dawn broke, they sought out Jesus, exclaiming when they found him, "Everyone is looking for you!" (Mark 1: 37). We too can get so caught up in the busyness of ministry that we forget to be still. We forget that we are to serve in the supply of the Spirit, not our own power. But the time will come when we learn that we cannot sustain the pace we have set for ourselves. We cannot manage apart from the Source.

Henri Nouwen writes, "A certain unavailability is essential for the spiritual life of the (leader)." It prompts the question: Whom would we be if communion were to shape our understanding of leadership?

Food for the Journey
- Psalm 42, As a deer longs
- Romans 8:18-39, The Spirit Intercedes
- Mark 1:35-39, Alone with the Father
- John 15, Abide with me

Journey Questions
1. Jesus made time to be with the Father even if it meant getting up before dawn. When do you spend time with the Father?
2. What practices help you to "abide" with Jesus and commune with the Father?
3. In what ways do you think that communion with God directs and shapes our intercession for others?
4. Do you agree or disagree with Nouwen that "a certain unavailability" for spiritual leaders is essential? Why?

Journey Practice: Silence and Solitude
The old Reformation hymn asks "O Lord how shall I meet you, how welcome you aright?" Carmelite Reformer and mystic Teresa of Avila advises us to "settle ourselves in stillness and we will come upon him in ourselves." Perhaps she had been thinking of the Psalmist charge to "Be still and know that I am God" (46:10). Yet how many still moments do we truly have in our lives? Our calendars reflect the craziness of our lives. This week, allow yourself some time apart with God in Christ, a daily moment of stillness simply to be and delight yourself in the Lord.

Prayer for the Journey
I ask you, Lord Jesus, to develop in me, your lover,
an immeasurable urge toward you,
an affection that is unbounded,
a longing that is unrestrained,
a fervor that throws discretion to the winds!
The more worthwhile our love for you,
all the more pressing does it become.
Reason cannot hold it in check,
fear does not make it tremble,
wise judgment does not temper it.
Richard Rolle

WHO DO YOU SAY THAT I AM?

But who do you say that I am?
Jesus (Matthew 16:13-20)

"But who do you say that I am?" Jesus asked.
"You are the Messiah, the Son of the living God!" Peter answered.

There. He had said it. There was no going back. It was one thing to think it, but entirely different to own it by saying it out loud. Daring to name the truth out loud moves us from an expression of faith that is private and personal to one that is public and communal.

Peter was the first of the disciples to name Jesus as the Messiah, the Christ. And for his faith, Jesus named him Peter (meaning "rock") and gave him the keys of the kingdom: "On this rock, I will build my church." Even so, Peter's relationship with Jesus was never a smooth one. No sooner had he been praised then Jesus was telling him to "Get behind me, Satan." This said in response to Peter's protective reaction to Jesus' foretelling of his crucifixion. You can feel the sting in the words. You can imagine the disciples' relief that the words were not directed at them, as well as their pain for Peter's disgrace.

Commitment always brings with it risk and vulnerability. It demands that we confront our fears of making a mistake (for we will always make mistakes on this life's journey). We will be tested. There will be trials. What we believe about God influences our ability to trust in the face of the unknown. To name Jesus as the Messiah demands surrender to God's call and claim upon our lives.

As Marjorie Bankson in *The Soul of Our Leadership* notes, "Deep within us is planted the seed of new creation—dreams for a better world and wild hope that our dreams can be realized." But for this seed to grow, for our dreams to be realized, we need to step out in faith. Heeding God's call requires going public with the call we carry deep in our hearts. Risk invariably involves confronting the status quo, within ourselves and others. Only then can we articulate the truth within us and embody God's call in our life and living.

Food for the Journey
- Deuteronomy 6:4-9, The Shema
- I Corinthians 1:17-25, I preach Christ crucified
- Matthew 16:13-20, Who do you say that I am?

Journey Questions
1. How do you respond to Jesus' question "who do people say that I am"? What does it mean to claim him as the Messiah, the Son of the Living God?
2. What gift is God calling you to share in this season?
3. What risks are involved? What fears do you need to confront?
4. How is God calling you to embody the truth that is within you?

Journey Practice: Give Testimony
What do you believe? The question Jesus put before the disciples he also puts before us: "Who do you say that I am?" Ultimately, each one of us must answer Jesus' question for ourselves.

In our pluralistic age, many of us shy away from talking about our faith, failing to recognize how our world hungers for our testimony. This next week, share your faith with a friend or family member. It doesn't have to be a stranger. Begin with those you know and give testimony to the faith that is within us.

Prayer for the Journey
God be with those who explore in the cause of understanding;
whose search takes them far from what is familiar and comfortable
and leads them into danger or terrifying loneliness.
Let us try to understand their sometimes strange or difficult ways;
their confronting or unusual language;
the uncommon life of their emotions,
for they have been affected and shaped and changed by their struggle
at the frontiers of a wild darkness,
just as we may be affected, shaped and changed
by the insights they bring back to us. Bless them with strength and peace. Amen.
Michael Leunig, <u>A Common Prayer</u>

TRANSFIGURED!

There Jesus was transfigured before them.
Matthew 17:2

What a moment—Jesus transfigured on the mountaintop! Literally changed before Peter and James and John eyes, face shining like the sun, his clothing white as light. And he wasn't alone: there were two men with him, two men they had never seen before, yet somehow the disciples knew who they were.

Peter's first response is to offer to build three booths to provide shelter for Jesus, Moses and Elijah. He was trying to be helpful, even as he sought to contain his anxiety over the sight before him. (In fairness, there was precedent. The booths, or tabernacles, had been used in the wilderness to contain the Holy One. Peter, whether consciously or not, wanted to contain these three awe-inspiring (read terrifying) figures.)

But before he could do anything, "a cloud came out and overshadowed them; and they were afraid as they entered the cloud. And a voice came out of the cloud saying, 'This is my beloved Son, my chosen, listen to him!'"

Whey they finally had the courage to look up, "they no longer saw anyone with them but Jesus only." No cloud. No voice. No Moses. No Elijah. Jesus only. There was no need for booths. Nor was there any need to contain them. They could not be contained.

Revelation is like that. There is that moment when heaven and earth meet, when *chronos* and *kairos* time intersect, and you enter that "thin place." Revelation brings with it ambivalence and uncertainty, possibility and potential danger. This is the way that new vision is born: when we are left with Jesus only.

He was all the disciples needed. He is all any of us ever need, but all too often we find his presence overwhelming. We don't know how to respond. So we try to contain him, like Peter, but not always in a booth; we try to compartmentalize God into the structures of our day. If we are to learn anything from the Transfiguration, it is that we cannot contain God. God's revelation will prevail. We need only trust ourselves, our very lives, to God's care and call.

Food for the Journey
- Hebrews 12:1-13, Jesus only
- Matthew 17:1-13, The Transfiguration

Journey Questions
1. How does the Transfiguration inform your understanding of call?
2. What has God revealed to your heart?
3. What it does it mean to focus on Jesus?

Journey Practice: The Heart of Worship
"Therefore, I urge you, brothers and sisters, in view of God's mercy, to offer your bodies as a living sacrifice, holy and pleasing to God—this is true worship" (Romans 12:1).

The heart of worship is to seek to know and love God with the whole of our lives. The apostle Paul reminds us that true worship is the offering of our very selves. Come before God with an open heart and listening ear. Ponder the question, "What do I value most?" Then answer the question from the perspective of those closest to you and from the perspective of God. What do you learn about yourself through their eyes? What did you learn about yourself through God's eyes? In what ways does your life reflect "true worship" born of offering yourself as a "living sacrifice"? In what ways do you find that you have failed to fully worship God? How might what you worship need to change?

Prayer for the Journey
God of life and glory,
your Son was revealed in splendor
before he suffered death upon the cross;
grant that we, beholding his majesty,
may be strengthened to follow him
and be changed into his likeness from glory to glory;
for he lives and reigns with you and the Holy Spirit,
one God now and for ever. Amen.
Book of Common Prayer

WOE TO YOU, SCRIBES AND PHARISEES!

A leader is a person who must take special responsibility for what's going on inside him or herself, inside his or her consciousness, lest the act of leadership create more harm than good.
Parker Palmer

"Woe to you, scribes and Pharisees, *hypocrites!*" These are harsh words, words that we would prefer to have directed at someone other than ourselves. But it seems to me Jesus' words to the Pharisees bring home those things within each one of us that need addressing. Things like enmity, strife, jealousy, anger, selfishness, dissension, and envy.

Seen in this context, conflict is an opportunity for getting our lives back on track with God and one another. Conflict calls us to let the power of the gospel take hold of us that the Spirit might break in and nurture the fruits of the Spirit: love, joy, peace, patience, kindness, goodness, gentleness, and self- control within us. Woe, indeed, to the scribe and Pharisee that dwells within each one of us.

The contrast between the defensive responses of the scribes and Pharisees and God's chosen leaders is dramatic. I am reminded of the prophet Isaiah when he first encountered the awesome majesty of God: "Woe is me! [...] For I am a man of unclean lips" (Isaiah 6:5). Similarly, I am reminded of Simon Peter, weary and discouraged after a night on the boat with no catch, when he first met Jesus said, "Go away from me, Lord, for I am a sinful man" (Luke 5:8). In their humility, neither man felt deserving of God's attention. They knew the condition of their souls and did not project their brokenness onto others. Both men took responsibility for what was going on inside himself, one of the first prerequisites for receiving God's call.

Of course, there are times our acts of faithfulness will result in conflict. In such times, we will encounter rejection and even persecution as Jesus did. As with Joshua, God calls us "to be strong and courageous" in the face of opposition (Joshua 1:6). This can be easier said than done. But God's promise is to be always with us, especially in times of challenge.

Indeed, God uses conflict to shape and form us more deeply in his image. The Apostle Paul understood this when he called us to "rejoice in our sufferings, because we know that suffering produces perseverance, perseverance, character, and character hope. And hope does not disappoint us because God has poured his love into our hearts by the Holy Spirit whom he has given us" (Romans 5:3-5).

Next time you find yourself in conflict, ask first what role you have played in creating it. If your role is born of God's call, then trust the outcome to God, allowing God to use it to develop more fully your character in Christ.

Food for the Journey
- Joshua 1, Be strong and courageous
- Romans 5:1-5, Suffering, endurance, hope
- Matthew 23:23-26, Woe to you, scribes and Pharisees

Journey Questions
1. Can you think of a time when you have behaved as a scribe or a Pharisee?
2. How do family-of-origin issues influence how you deal with conflict? How does Jesus model a better way?
3. How does God use conflict to more fully develop our character in Christ? Can you think of particular times when this was so in your own life?

Journey Practice: Seven Habits of Health Promoting Leaders
Take some time to reflect systemically on who you are as a leader, using these guiding questions from *The Seven Habits of Health Promoting Spiritual Leaders* (James Boyer, <u>Healthy Congregations</u>, 1998.):

1. *Spiritual Grounding*
   a. The spiritual theme(s) I would give to the past year is:
   b. My most powerful spiritual experience in the past year was:
   c. My most difficult struggle in the past year was:
2. *Manage Anxiety*
   a. When I become anxious, I: internally and externally:
   b. What I do to calm myself:
   c. My main anxiety triggers are:
   d. Anxiety triggers I have/am overcoming are:
3. *Take Stands and Stay Connected*
   a. Three things I know to be true and base my ministry on are:
   b. I struggle to stay connected:
   c. I feel good about holding the course on:
4. *Focus on Presence and Functioning*
   a. Something I learned/clarified about my functioning as a leader this year was:
   b. I maintain balance between under and overfunctioning by:
   c. When I lose my objectivity, I:

5. *Focus on Vision and Mission*
    a. I can get distracted from my/our vision by:
    b. I find my way back to my/our vision by:
    c. I keep my mission and vision before the congregation by:
6. *Focus on Strengths*
    a. I am proud of our congregation's strengths in the area of:
    b. I look forward to developing/strengthening this coming year in the areas of:
7. *Challenges Self and Others*
    a. I hope to grow in the following areas this coming year:
    b. I would predict the greatest resistance to ..... this coming year:
    c. I think we need to challenge the congregation to:

Prayer for the Journey
O Lord, my God,
Form me more fully into your likeness.
Use the circumstances and interaction of this day to form your will in me.
From the frustrations of this day form peace.
From the joys of this day form strength.
From the struggles of this day form courage.
From the beauties of this day form love.
In the name of Jesus Christ who is all peace and strength and courage and love. Amen.
Richard Foster

JERUSALEM, JERUSALEM!

O Jerusalem, Jerusalem, the city that kills the prophets and stones God's messengers! How often I have wanted to gather your children together as a hen protects her chicks beneath her wings, but you wouldn't let me.
Jesus (Matthew 23:37)

Jesus is one step closer to Jerusalem, one step closer to the cross. He is moving from Galilee towards the center of power, Jerusalem. He knows he is on the road to his death. He knows that his ministry has caused the foreign rulers and the religious leaders of the Temple to want to kill him.

Sympathetic Pharisees have come to warn Jesus of danger. "Get away from here, for Herod wants to kill you." They knew that the centers of power are starting to fear Jesus message. Jesus, instead of turning back, sends a cryptic message to Herod: "Go and tell that Fox for me, 'Listen, I am casting out demons and performing cures today and tomorrow, and on the third day I finish my work.'"

In this way, Jesus turns his face to the cross! He has been warned by the forces of destruction and the powers of this world. His response it to lament over Jerusalem: "O Jerusalem, Jerusalem, the city that kills the prophets and stones those who are sent to it! How often have I desired to gather your children together as a hen gathers her brood under her wings, and you were not willing!" With these words, he reaches out with a motherly love to embrace Jerusalem, to grieve over the destruction and harm that is to come from choosing this world's way.

In this moment, Jesus again reflects the depth of God's love for us, even as he exposes the truth about our complicity with the powers and principalities of our day. As we travel towards Jerusalem and the cross, Jesus' desire to gather us in like a mother hen invites us into the divine embrace that we might be healed.

Food for the Journey
- Daniel 10: 1-21, Conflict of nations and heavenly powers
- Romans 8:18-30, present suffering and future glory
- Matthew 23:1-39, Luke 13:31-35, O Jerusalem, Jerusalem

Journey Questions
1. With whom do you most identify with in the gospel passage? Be honest.
2. How does Jesus' response inform our response to the powers and principalities of our day?
3. Are you able to allow Jesus to draw you into the shelter of the divine embrace? Why or why not?

Journey Practice: Weep, Worship & Walk
Jesus' grief for Jerusalem is palpable. He loves his people—even those with whom he disagrees. As he prepares to journey to the cross, he laments over his inability to bear truth and life. Is there anything that God is calling you to weep over, to grieve, in your community?

This next week, take time in prayer to:
- Weep over the brokenness you experience;
- Worship God as you make confession for both yourself and your community; and
- Walk the community offering prayer.

Prayer for the Journey
Scripture admonishes believers in God to: "Pray for the peace [shalom] of Jerusalem" (Psalm 122:6). This next week, prayerfully read Psalm 122 and then offer prayers for the Shalom of your community.

The Journey:
Growing Up in Christ

Living the Sacramental Life

LIVING THE SACRAMENTAL LIFE

Blessed are you when people revile you and persecute you and utter all kinds of evil against you falsely on my account. Rejoice and be glad, for your reward is great in heaven.
Matthew 5:11, The Beatitudes

Reviled and persecuted. Such is the way of the cross. Jesus is clear: we are to rejoice and be glad in response. As is always the case, the choice is ours to make. Will we choose to repay vengeance with vengeance, or will we follow Jesus?

The sacramental life is about responding to the world (in all its brokenness) with love and compassion. What began with the grace-saturated embrace, refined through the love and testing of the wilderness, and articulated through engagement now finds fullness of expression through the way of the cross. Death precedes resurrection. Costly sacrifice gives way to new life.

In and throughout the sacramental life, Jesus embodies compassion... even at the cost of his life. He becomes a living sacrament for us. "This is my body, given for you," he tells the disciples. "This is my blood poured out for the new covenant."

Are we ready to do the same?

FROM HOSANNA TO CRUCIFY!

*In your relationships with one another, have the same mind as Christ
Jesus: Who, being in very nature God, did not consider equality with
God something to be used to his own advantage; rather, he emptied
himself taking the very nature of a servant, being made in human
likeness. And being found in appearance as a man, he humbled
himself by becoming obedient to death—even death on a cross!*
Philippians 2: 5-8

"Hosanna! Save us!" They shouted as he road forth into Jerusalem. And
save them he did… just not in the way expected. Salvation came in the
form of death on a cross, not the overturning of those in power. It came in
the emptying of divine prerogative and power. The Apostle Paul captured
this in Philippians 2 when he wrote: "he emptied [… and] humbled
himself by becoming obedient to death—even death on a cross!"

He who was merciful and pure of heart, he who was a peacemaker sent
from God, was a threat to the established orders and for that he was
crucified. Even those who wanted change wanted it on their terms—
human terms—not God's terms. He betrayed their expectations and so
their shouts of *Hosanna* became cries of *Crucify*!

Triumphant entry becomes betrayal. Trial results in crucifixion. In the
space of one week, he who was hailed with shouts of joy is sent to his
death. Betrayed with a kiss. Denied by another. Abandoned by all but one
disciple and the women. He is scourged and mocked. Nailed to a cross.
Dead.

It is not a pretty picture, but we dare not stand at a distance. Each one of
us must acknowledge our own complicity in his betrayal. Each one of us
must deal with the division within ourselves: God's way or our way?

Let us not fool ourselves into thinking we would be different. We too must
ask, "Is it I, Lord?" As poet Ann Weems writes, "the only road to Easter
morning is through the unrelenting shadows of that Friday."

Food for the Journey
- Isaiah 58:1-12, Suffering servant
- Philippians 2:12-18, Work out your salvation with fear and trembling
- Mark 14-16, The journey to the cross

Journey Questions
1. As you enter into what has become known as the Holy Week narrative, what forms of resistance do you encounter within yourself?
2. Where in your life do you struggle with choosing between God's way and your way?
3. How is God calling you to work out your salvation with fear and trembling?

Journey Practice: Were You There?
The old spiritual asks us:

"Were you there when they crucified my Lord?
Were you there when they crucified my Lord?
Oh, sometimes it causes me to tremble, tremble, tremble.
Were you there when they crucified my Lord?"

This week, choose one of the disciples or women or participants in the Holy Week narrative and enter his or her story. Allow yourself to settle into your humanity: your own cries of hosanna, your own times at table with the Lord, your own Gethsemanes, your own betrayals, your own trials, your own crucifixions. Allow yourself to engage—body, mind, emotions, and spirit—in their experience of the movement from Palm Sunday to Maundy Thursday, to Good Friday, to Holy Saturday, to Easter Sunday. Feel what they felt—don't shy away from the pain. Allow the emotions to inform your journey. Then offer to God in prayer any insights you have received from this time apart.

Prayer for the Journey
Empty me, Lord, of all that holds me back from this journey.
Empty me of all that holds me apart from you.
Most especially, empty me of my fears and my resistance.
So that I may have the same mind as Jesus
who choose not divine prerogative but the way of the cross.
Holy is this journey. Holy are you. Holy am I in you.

UPPER ROOM INSTRUCTIONS:
LOVE ONE ANOTHER

Love one another as I have loved you.
Jesus (John 13:34)

Spend time in the Upper Room with Jesus, and you cannot help but be overcome by his love for us. The words of one hymn in particular speak to the depth of his love: "O love so broad, so deep, so high that God, the Son of God, should take my mortal form for mortals' sake."

How much intensity of feeling can the human heart take? How much can God's heart take? Can we even imagine our Lord's loneliness, his anguish, his desire to get through the baptism with which he was to be baptized?

And what of us? Is it even possible for us to love one another as he has loved us? Love for Jesus meant loneliness, anguish and ultimately death on a cross. If we're honest, we recoil from such a costly love. Yet I wonder if our fear of pain and death gets in the way of our loving. I wonder if true cost of drawing near to the cross is not dying, but rather coming alive in Christ.

The spiritual journey is full of paradoxes. In our weakness, we come to know God's strength. Out of our brokenness, we are made whole. Through death comes life. Perhaps paradox is the means by which we will come to understand how to love one another as Jesus has loved us. "Lamb of God, you take away the sins of the world! Have mercy on me, a sinner." We pray as we give thanks for love so deep, so broad, so high that God should become incarnate and chose the way of the cross—for our sake!

But what does this mean for us in a practical level? Teresa of Avila put it this way:
"Christ has no body but yours,
No hands, no feet on earth but yours,
Yours are the eyes with which he looks compassion on this world,
Yours are the feet with which he walks to do good,
Yours are the hands, with which he blesses all the world.
Yours are the hands, yours are the feet,
Yours are the eyes, you are his body.
Christ has no body now but yours,
No hands, no feet on earth but yours,

119

Yours are the eyes with which he looks compassion on this world.
Christ has no body now on earth but yours."

Becoming like Jesus: this is the means by which we are set free to love as
Christ as loved us. This is the means by which we become Christ for the
world.

Food for the Journey
- Jeremiah 31:30-34, A new covenant
- I Corinthians 13, The greatest of these is love
- John 14:34, A new commandment

Journey Questions
1. How does Paul define love in I Corinthians 13?
2. How does Jesus model love in the Upper Room?
3. What is Jesus asking when he commands us to love another?

Journey Practice: Love One Another
Earlier in *The Journey*, we engaged the "one anothers." Now we return to
them to ponder Jesus' call to love one another in the context of the
sacramental life. Below is the complete listing of verse references to the
Greek word *allenlous* (translated as "one another" or "each other"). Pray
through the "one anothers" below, and ponder how they inform your
understanding of Jesus' commandment to "love one another."

- Mark 9:50 "... Have salt in yourselves, and **be at peace with each other.**"
- John 13:14 "Now that I, your Lord and Teacher, have washed your feet, you also should **wash one another's feet.**"
- John 13:34 "A new command I give you: **Love one another.** As I have loved you, so you must **love one another.**"
- John 15:12 "My command is this: **Love each other** as I have loved you."
- John 15:17 "This is my command: **Love each other.**"
- Romans 12:10 **Be devoted to one another** with mutual affection. **Honor one another above yourselves.**
- Romans 12:16 **Live in harmony with one another.**
- Romans 13:8 Let no debt remain outstanding, except the continuing debt to **love one another**, for whoever loves others has fulfilled the law.

- Romans 14:13 Therefore let us **stop passing judgment on one another**...
- Romans 15:7 **Accept one another**, then, just as Christ accepted you, in order to bring praise to God.
- Rom. 16:16 **Greet one another with a holy kiss**...
- 1 Corinthians 1:10 I appeal to you, brothers and sisters, in the name of our Lord Jesus Christ, that all of you **agree with one another** so that there may be no divisions among you and that you may be perfectly united in mind and thought.
- 1 Corinthians 11:33 So then, my brothers and sisters, when you come together to eat, **wait for each other.**
- 1 Corinthians 12:24-25 ...But God has combined the members of the body and has given greater honor to the parts that lacked it, so that there should be no division in the body, but that its parts should **have equal concern for each other.**
- 1 Corinthians 16:20 ...**Greet one another with a holy kiss.**
- 2 Corinthians 13:12 **Greet one another with a holy kiss.**
- Galatians 5:13 ..But do not use your freedom to indulge the sinful nature; rather, **serve one another in love**.
- Galatians 5:26 **Let us not become conceited, provoking and envying each other.**
- Galatians 6:2 **Carry each other's burdens**, and in this way you will fulfill the law of Christ.
- Ephesians 4:2 Be completely humble and gentle; be patient, **bearing with one another** in love.
- Ephesians 4:32 **Be kind and compassionate to one another, forgiving each other**, just as in Christ God forgave you.
- Ephesians 5:19 **Speak to one another with psalms, hymns and spiritual songs**...
- Ephesians 5:21 **Submit to one another** out of reverence for Christ.
- Colossians 3:9 **Do not lie to each other**, since you have taken off your old self with its practices
- Colossians 3:13 **Bear with each other** and **forgive whatever grievances you may have against one another**...
- Colossians 3:16 Let the word of Christ dwell in you richly as you **teach and admonish one another** with all wisdom, and as you sing psalms, hymns and spiritual songs with gratitude in your hearts to God.

- 1 Thessalonians 4:9 Now about your mutual love we do not need to write to you, for you yourselves have been taught by God to **love each other.**
- 1 Thessalonians 4:18 Therefore **encourage each other** with these words.
- 1 Thessalonians 5:11 Therefore **encourage one another** and **build each other up,** just as in fact you are doing.
- 1 Thessalonians 5:13 ...**Live in peace with each other.**
- 1 Thessalonians 5:15 Make sure that nobody pays back wrong for wrong, but always try to **be kind to each other** and to everyone else.
- Hebrews 3:13 But **encourage one another** daily, as long as it is called Today, so that none of you may be hardened by sin's deceitfulness.
- Hebrews 10:24-25 And let us consider how we may **spur one another on toward love and good deeds.** Let us not give up meeting together, as some are in the habit of doing, but let us encourage one another and all the more as you see the Day approaching.
- Hebrews 13:1 Keep on **loving each other** as brothers and sisters.
- James 4:11 Brothers and sisters, **do not slander one another...**
- James 5:9 **Don't grumble against each other,** brothers and sisters, or you will be judged...
- James 5:16 Therefore **confess your sins to each other** and **pray for each other** so that you may be healed...
- 1 John 3:11 This is the message you heard from the beginning: **We should love one another.**
- 1 John 3:23 And this is his command: to believe in the name of his Son, Jesus Christ, and to **love one another** as he commanded us.
- 1 John 4:7 Dear friends, let us **love one another,** for love comes from God...
- 1 John 4:11 Dear friends, since God so loved us, we also ought to **love one another.**
- 2 John. 1:5 ...I ask that we **love one another.**
- 1 Peter 1:22 Now that you have purified yourselves by obeying the truth so that you have sincere mutual affection, **love one another** deeply, from the heart.
- 1 Peter 3:8 Finally, all of you, **live in harmony with one another;** be sympathetic, **love one another,** be compassionate and humble.
- 1 Peter 4:8 Above all, **love each other** deeply, because love covers over a multitude of sins.

- 1 Peter 4:9 **Offer hospitality to one another without grumbling.**
- 1 Peter 5:5 ...All of you, **clothe yourselves with humility toward one another**, because, "God opposes the proud but gives grace to the humble."
- 1 Peter 5:14 **Greet one another with a kiss of love...**

Prayer for the Journey

Help us accept each other as Christ accepted us.
Teach us as sister, brother, each person to embrace.
Be present, Lord, among us and bring us to believe
We are ourselves accepted and meant to love and live.
Fred Kaan, 1975

IS IT I, LORD?

For there to be betrayal, there would have to be trust first.
Suzanne Collins, <u>The Hunger Games</u>

While we would prefer to remain focused on the commandment to love one another, the crucifixion narratives move us on to betrayal.

Betrayal. It is not something any of us likes to focus on, yet pondering betrayal is a part of the journey. What makes betrayal so painful is that it that "for there to be betrayal, there would have to be trust first." Someone who knows our heart, who knows our longings and character, chooses to act not in love, but instead hurt us and betray our trust in them.

Michael Card brilliantly captures the agony of betrayal in a song: "Only a friend can betray a friend, a stranger has nothing to gain, and only a friend comes close enough to ever cause so much pain." We can all attest to the pain of betrayal. But what about those times when we are a betrayer?

The question the disciples asked of themselves is a question we do well to ask, "Is it I, Lord? Is it I?" If we're really honest, there lies a Judas within each of us. While we look critically at Judas and regard him with a mixture of contempt and horror, you know and I know the truth. We are no different.

Take one of the other disciples. Would we have been braver than those who had forsaken him and fled? Would we have had the courage to admit what Peter denied, that we had been with Jesus? Would I, sitting at the table, have felt the same stab of conscience at Jesus' statement: "One of you will betray me"? Yes. And that must mean that there was not a single one of them who had not had the thought earlier. So it was not Judas alone who betrayed Jesus—it was all of them. It is all of us. It is me. It is you.

We do well, then, to remember that Judas did not leave the Upper Room until after the supper. With the other disciples, he heard Jesus' words ("This is my body, given for you"), and he ate the bread. He heard the words "This is my blood of the new covenant", and he drank the wine. Jesus did not cast him out or turn him away. So also, he was present at the foot washing. All four gospels agree that Judas was not asked to leave! How are we to understand this?

On the night he was betrayed, Jesus tells us that he loves his own and will keep on loving them right to the end. Judas was one of Jesus' own! And, in spite of everything, he never ceased to be one of Jesus' own. Jesus loved him to the end.

One more piece of mystery: In I Corinthians, Paul describes the resurrection appearances. He says that Jesus "appeared to the twelve." But how could this be? Who was the twelfth person? It could not have been Matthias. He was not appointed to the twelve until after the Ascension. It could not have been Paul himself, because Paul mentions his own resurrection appearance a verse or two later. So who could it be? Judas was an apostle, and he was one of the twelve. He never ceased to be that.

But, you ask, did not Jesus say that it would be better if the one who betrayed him had never been born? Does not the Fourth Gospel describe Judas as a "son of perdition" and one "doomed to destruction"? No doubt these words point forward to the terrible way that Judas died, yet scripture also seems to indicate hope. Could not the one who received Judas at the table, even at the moment of betrayal, still forgive him and receive him?

Don't ask me how Jesus could appear to Judas when Judas was already dead. I don't know. Maybe Paul got it wrong. But this I do know: Jesus loved him to the end. So also, he loves us to the end, not only in our faithfulness but also in our betrayals. Whatever we have done, might have done, think you once did, or fear that you might do, his amazing love holds you and will go on holding you, up to death, and beyond.

Food for the Journey
- Psalm 124, If the Lord had not been at our side
- I Corinthians 15:1-11, He appeared to the twelve
- Matthew 26:17-30, Is it I, Lord?

Journey Questions
1. What experiences have affected your ability to give and receive forgiveness?
2. When have you last tasted the joy of forgiveness? What was that like for you?
3. When did you last seek forgiveness?

Journey Practice: Pondering Betrayal

Take some time this week to ponder the betrayals in your life: those times when you've been betrayed and those times when you have been the betrayer. Be candid with yourself. Then ponder how God is calling you to apologize for those times when you have betrayed another. When pondering the experience of being betrayed, ask yourself how God is calling you to forgive. Jesus modeled this from the cross when he asked God the Father to forgive us (each and every one of us).

Spend some time in the Word daring to ponder the ways in which you have betrayed Jesus. Seek God's forgiveness and allow yourself to be emptied of all that holds you apart from God.

Prayer for the Journey

Christ our victim, whose beauty was disfigured
and whose body torn upon the cross: open wide your arms
to embrace our tortured world, that we may not turn away our eyes,
but abandon ourselves to your mercy. Amen.

All Desires Known

GETHSEMANE: WATCH WITH ME

This is the place of prayer where God calls en route to the cross. God invites us to the silence and solitude of the garden to prepare us for the darkness of the cross. Here we are called to remember who and whose we are. Here we ponder our core identity in Christ, our character, our call to live the sacramental life.

Of course, Biblical remembering is not merely a mental activity of recollection, but an entering into the narrative with our whole self. Anyone who dared to see *The Passion of the Christ* knows the pain involved in entering into this part of our story. But enter we must if we are to be conformed to the image of Christ.

We live in a society that fears sacrifice of self, seeking instead quick fixes that only lead to deeper pain. Giving sacrificially demands that we enter into dark places and remain vulnerable and open. Have you ever noticed how the most significant events in Jesus' life occur in the darkness: his birth, his arrest, his death, and his resurrection?

The mystics have long known the gift born of the dark night of the soul. For Teresa of Avila, the dark night was a profound gift of God in which she came to encounter God at the center of her soul. John of the Cross believed that the purpose of the dark night was to purge us of all that holds us apart from God. But where do we begin?

Thomas Merton notes that darkness comes when we allow God to strip away our false selves and make us into the persons we're meant to be. This is uncomfortable work. Entering into the crucible of darkness involves painful confrontation with those parts of ourselves that are not of God: our disordered affections and unhealthy attachments. It can be difficult to believe in resurrection when you stand in the hollow carved out by death. But the mystery of our faith is that death precedes resurrection.

This is an invitation to enter into holy darkness. Therein lies God's "Eastering" of your soul. This is something that cannot be orchestrated, controlled or forced. It can only be lived.

Food for the Journey: The Gethsemane accounts
- Matthew 26:36-48
- Mark 14:32-41
- Luke 22:39-46

Journey Questions
1. How does Jesus' time in Gethsemane inform how we are to yield to God's will for our lives?
2. How have you "watched" with Jesus and others in their time of need?
3. What would you need to surrender in order to be able to pray with Jesus to the Father "Not my will, but your will be done"?

Journey Practice: Relinquishment
Pray to recognize and relinquish anything that takes priority over God's will. This is at the heart of Jesus' prayer in Gethsemane where he prayed to take away the cup: "Nevertheless, not my will, but thine." This prayer is often called the "prayer of relinquishment," as it calls us to let go of our will and desire, surrendering our life to God alone. As you enter into this prayer, ask God to move in your will so that you follow in the way of the cross.

Note: If you can't pray this prayer, than pray for the desire to pray this prayer.

A Prayer of Relinquishment
Today, O Lord, I yield myself to you.
May your will be my delight.
May your way have perfect sway in me.
May your love be the pattern of my living.
I surrender to you: my hopes, my dreams, my ambitions.
Do with them what your will, when you will, as you will.
I place into your loving care: my family, my friends, my future.
Care for them with a care that I can never give.
I release into your hands:
my need to control, my craving for status, my fear of obscurity.
Eradicate the evil, purify the good, and establish your kingdom on earth.
For Jesus' sake. Amen.
Richard Foster

DENIAL

We may ignore, but nowhere can we evade, the presence of God.
CS Lewis, <u>Letters of Malcolm</u>

He was the first of the disciples to acknowledge him as the Messiah, the Christ. In response, Jesus gave him the keys of the kingdom and named him Peter: "On this rock, I will build my church." Yet because of his desire to protect Jesus from the cross and to keep him from harm, Peter is also the first to be rebuked for his misunderstanding of what it means to be the Messiah. "Get behind me, Satan!" was Jesus' response to Peter's reaction to the cross. You can feel the sting in the words. You can imagine the other disciples' relief that Jesus' words were directed to Peter and not at them. You can feel their pain for Peter's disgrace.

Peter was a man of deep feelings and commitment. Such was his love of Jesus that he followed him into the inner courtyard of the High Priest's home. It is there that he denied him, not once but three times, as Jesus predicted. He denied knowing his Lord and Master. He denied being one of the Twelve. He denied any and all connections: "Woman, I do not know the man!" And then the cock crowed the third time.

Even after the resurrection, the shame of his betrayal stayed with him. He had been called by Jesus to build his church. But all that he felt capable of doing was to return to his nets and boat, to run from Jesus' call, a call that reminded him of his failure to support the man he loved and stand by him in his time of trial.

Jesus, however, had other plans for Peter. With breakfast on the beach, he loves him back into wholeness and gives him his marching orders: "Tend my flock. Feed my lambs." Three times, he asks Peter: "Do you love me?" Three times, Peter responds. But, we get ahead of the narrative.

So often, we allow our failures—our denials—to get in the way of Jesus' love and call. Jesus reached out to Peter in his pain and brokenness. He forgave his past and offered him a future. From the cross, he does the same for us.: "Father, forgive them for they know not what they do."

Don't let the pain of your past hold you back from the divine embrace and the call to live the sacramental life.

Food for the Journey

- Matthew 26:31-35; Mark 14:27-31; Luke 22:31-34, Jesus predicts Peter's Denial
- Mark 14: 66-72; Luke 22:54-62; John 18:15-27, Peter's denial

Journey Questions

1. Facing our denials is never easy. But when we fail to acknowledge them, they haunt us as Peter's denial haunted him. Is the pain of denial holding you apart from God's love and call?
2. It has been said that forgiveness is another word for letting go. Is there something that God is calling you to forgive yourself for, to let go of, in order that you may more fully live the sacramental life?
3. Peter tried to evade the risen Christ by returning to his boat and nets. Are there any ways in which you are trying to evade God through your work or some other aspect of your life? How is God seeking you?

Journey Practice: "FACE"

In his book *Shadow Dancing*, David Richo creates an acronym for the ego's FACE: Fear, Attachment, Control and Entitlement. In preparation for reclaiming your core identity in Christ, prayerfully reflect on those places in your life where God is calling you to move from:

- **F**ear to curiosity;
- **A**ttachment to letting go;
- **C**ontrol to trust;
- **E**ntitlement to humility.

Ask yourself, how will I nurture curiosity, practice letting go, more fully trust God, model humility? Commit yourself to one aspect of reclaiming by sharing with a friend or family member where you are feeling God's call. Be aware that such shifts will initially feel uncomfortable, even odd. You may feel awkward and disoriented as you let go of tired and stale patterns in your life. But never doubt that as you claim your God-given FACE, you will experience the very authenticity you have been yearning for in Christ. Such authenticity is the source of spiritual authority and joy. Blessings as you FACE yourself!

Prayer for the Journey

How then shall we live?
How shall this faith take flesh in the world?
The cross? We will take it.
The bread? We will break it.
The pain? We will bear it.
The joy? We will share it.
The Gospel? We will live it.
The love? We will give it.
The light? We will cherish it.
The darkness? God shall perish it.
Iona Community Worship Book

WHAT IS TRUTH?

I am the way, the truth, and the life.
Jesus

"What is truth?" Pilate asked Jesus before he washed his hands of the whole affair and sent him forth to be crucified. Jesus never answered him. He simply stood there before him. He knew that Pilate already had the answer in his heart. The real question was whether he would act upon the truth within him or allow his decision to be driven by political survival tactics.

Truth was an issue for the early church as well. The Apostle Paul continually charged believers to "speak the truth in love that they might grow up in every way into Christ, from whom the whole body is joined" (Ephesians 4:15). But not everyone responded as the apostle would have wished. Indeed, his relations with the Galatians became so strained that he wrote them asking "Have I become your enemy by telling you to the truth?" (Galatians 4:16).

My own experience is that there are those who will seek the truth, whatever the cost, while there are others who fear the truth even when it would set them free. The cost feels too great. We are afraid we will hurt others. We are afraid that we will be hurt. The problem is that when we refuse to deal with the truth straight forwardly, it demands our attention in other ways. Tension begins to take hold of our lives. Relationships, once so precious, become brittle and break. Our health is affected. The freedom and ease with which we once approached life is replaced by a sense of being weighed down and burdened. In the end, we are forced to deal with the truth one way or another. We know what Pilate decided. But what will decide?

Food for the Journey
- Ephesians 4:1-16, Unity in the Body of Christ
- Galatians 4:8-20, Paul's concern for the Galatians
- John 14:1-14, Jesus is the way, the truth, and the life
- John 18:28-40; Matthew 27:11-18, 20-23; Mark 15:2-15; Luke 23:2, 3, 18-25, Jesus before Pilate

Journey Questions

1. Pilate asked, "What is truth?" How do you answer that question?
2. What does it mean for Jesus to say that he is "the way, the truth, and the life"?
3. Is there a truth that God is calling you to grapple with in your life?

Journey Practice: Truth-telling

As Christians, our understanding of truth is born out of our relationship with God in Christ. The call to practice truth telling is not simply a moral mandate, it is way of living born out of following the One who is "the way, the *truth*, and the life." We live in a culture that often reduces truth to that which is convenient. Spinning is the norm. Cutting corners and cheating are common practice. Engaging in gossip and rumors abound. At best, our culture exemplifies a sliding scale of honesty. But we are called to follow the example of Jesus, who reminds us that truth telling begins with simply letting our "yes be yes and (our) no be no" (Matthew 5:37).

In order to speak the truth, we must first be truthful. On a daily basis we must work to avoid habits that lead to exaggerating, rationalizing and gossiping, all to make ourselves look better. In our daily examination of self, we need to confront the lies we tell. This includes both the tapes we play inside our heads that leave us feeling worthless, inadequate and unloved, as well those lies we tell ourselves to avoid confronting our sinfulness. Scripture is clear: the truth will set us free. But such freedom involves not only repentance and confession, but a daily dying of self that Christ might live in us.

Take some uninterrupted time to assess your honesty. Think back over the past week. Where have you been tempted to stretch the truth, take advantage of a privilege, break a commitment or gossip? What do you see about yourself? Where is it hardest for you to tell the truth? Write a prayer of confession or confess your sins to a trusted friend. Ask that friend to pray for you (*Spiritual Disciplines Handbook*, p. 202).

Prayer for the Journey

In order to be truthful, we must do more than speak the truth.
We must also hear the truth. We must also receive the truth.
We must also act upon the truth. We must also search for the truth.
The difficult truth. Within and around us. We must devote ourselves to truth.
Otherwise we are dishonest, and our lives are mistaken.
God grant us the strength and the courage to be truthful. Amen.
Michael Leunig, A Common Prayer

THE CROSS

*That which is Christ-like within us shall be crucified. It shall suffer
and be broken. And that which is Christ-like within us shall rise up.
It shall love and create.*
Michael Leunig

Death precedes resurrection. There is no way around it. Much as we might
want to leap from the triumphant entry to resurrection, it cannot be done.
Nor should we even try.

Jesus approached his death with a mixture of dread and yearning. "I have a
baptism to be baptized with, and how I am constrained until it is
accomplished" (Luke 12:50). While he entered into the fullness of our
humanity, in all our brokenness, it was only with his death that he
completed his kenotic descent into our sinful state. So full was his
identification that he could utter: "My God, my God, why have you
forsaken me?"

We live in a world where death dominates and is used as a means of power
and control. I speak here not just of physical death, but also of spiritual
death: a slow, painful eroding of the soul. Our Lord's death and
resurrection tells us that death no longer has the final word, that Jesus on
the cross claimed victory over *all* death once and for all.

Yet we continue to allow our lives to be directed by death, rather than by
life. Perhaps that is because so much of life is lived in the face of death
that, deep down, we don't really believe that God is victorious over the
grave. Or, perhaps even closer to the truth, we don't believe forgiveness is
truly possible. We know that we are all one in sin, even as we are all one in
guilt. We struggle to believe that, for our sake, God "made him to be sin
who knew no sin" (II Corinthians 5:21).

The way of the cross requires trust. Trust in God. It involves long nights
in prayer while others fall asleep. It calls for surrender in our Gethsemanes:
"Not my will, but yours be done" (Luke 22:42). Sometimes our tears
become like blood the suffering is so great.

When we dare to follow in the way of the cross, we are set free to love
without restraint. We dare to embrace the pain within us that we might
encounter the fullness of life that God offers. We let go of the illusion that
life without the cross can lead to happiness and wholeness. We come to

134

understand that it is in the giving that we receive and in the letting go that life is given. It is then that we are ready to practice resurrection knowing "that which is Christ-like within us shall be crucified. It shall suffer and be broken. And that which is Christ-like within us shall rise up. It shall love and create." Praise be to God!

Food for the Journey
- Malachi 3:1-3, Refiner's fire
- Matthew 16:21-28, Take up your cross
- Luke 23:26-49, Jesus' crucifixion

Journey Questions
1. What is your experience of death? How does your experience of death shape your response to Jesus' death?
2. What does it mean for Jesus to call us to take up our cross and follow him?
3. How are you being called to entrust God with your life unto death?

Journey Practice: Crucifixion
1. Choose one of the gospel texts above to quietly and slowly read.
2. Take a few moments when you finish to sit quietly in God's presence.
3. Without trying to fix anything or figure anything out, allow yourself to experience God's love made known in Jesus through his sacrifice on the cross.
4. After resting in God's presence, invite God to help you start seeing and naming the experiences that have shaped you. What are the patterns underneath the behaviors that God is challenging you to name? Are there places in your life that need to be "crucified" that you might experience the power of God's resurrection? Are you aware of hidden patterns or even addictions that are hindering your spiritual journey? *Do not* allow this to become self-flagellation! Rather, invite God to lead you into a place of holy darkness from which God's new life may emerge.
5. Offer to God in prayer whatever is on your heart.

Prayer for the Journey
That which is Christ-like within us shall be crucified.
It shall suffer and be broken.
And that which is Christ-like within us shall rise up.
It shall love and create.
Michael Leunig, A Common Prayer

GOLGOTHA: IT IS FINISHED!

Everything in my life has brought me here.
Rainer Marie Rilke

"It is finished!" Jesus said, and with that uttered his last breath.

Golgotha invites us to journey into darkness, the darkness of the cross in which we are called to remember the events that shaped Jesus' last day: his last supper with the twelve, Gethsemane, Judas' betrayal followed by his arrest, the fleeing of the disciples, Peter's denial followed by the disciple's despair upon hearing the cock crow, his trial and scourging, the painful journey to Golgotha, his crucifixion, the ridicule of the crowd and the witness of the women with the beloved disciple at the foot of the cross, his death.

Of course, Biblical remembering is not merely a mental activity of recollection, but an entering into the narrative with our whole self. Anyone who dared to see *The Passion of the Christ* knows the pain involved in entering into this part of our story. But enter we must if we are to be conformed to the image of Christ.

We live in a society that fears the darkness of death, seeking instead quick fixes that only lead to deeper pain. Entering into darkness is never easy. But it is an essential part of the journey. Have you ever noticed how the most significant events in Jesus' life occur in darkness: his birth, his arrest, his death, and his resurrection?

The mystics have long known the gift born of the dark night of the soul. For Teresa of Avila, the dark night was a profound gift of God in which she came to encounter God at the center of her soul. John of the Cross believed that the purpose of the dark night was to purge us of all that holds us apart from God. But where do we begin?

Thomas Merton notes that darkness comes when we allow God to strip away our false selves and make us into the persons we're meant to be. This is uncomfortable work. Entering into the crucible of darkness involves painful confrontation with those parts of ourselves that are not of God: our disordered affections and unhealthy attachments. It can be difficult to believe in resurrection when you stand in the hollow carved out by death. But the mystery of our faith is that death precedes resurrection. The journey from death to new life is not something that cannot be orchestrated, controlled or forced. When we dare to claim all that we have been and are, it is then that we know that everything in our life has brought us here.

Food for the Journey: The Crucifixion
- Matthew 27:32-44
- Mark 15:22-32
- Luke 23:33-43
- John 19:17-24

Journey Questions
1. In what ways is God inviting you into the darkness of cross on your own journey?
2. What is God seeking to strip you of in this season that you might die to your false self and thereby rise with Christ into new life?
3. Is there anything God is asking you to die in order to more fully live the sacramental life?

Journey Practice: Prayer at the Cross
(Source: *The Spiritual Formation Bible*)
1. Read: Matthew 27:32-55
2. Imagine you are standing at Golgotha at the foot of the cross while Jesus is being crucified. Listen to the sound of the hammer pounding nails into the soft flesh, the thud of the cross as it is lifted into place. Look at the people there with you. Some are mocking, some weeping. What are you doing? Do you walk to others or keep to yourself? What are your thoughts and feelings as the sky grows dark and Jesus cries out?
3. Sing a hymn such as "Go to Dark Gethsemane" or "Were You There?" or "When I Survey the Wondrous Cross." What emotions do you experience as you sing? How have you encountered the reality of Jesus' crucifixion and death through these hymns?

Prayer for the Journey
God help us if our world should grow dark and there is no way of seeing or knowing.
Grant us courage and trust: to touch and be touched, to find our way onwards by feeling.
Amen.
Michael Leunig, A Common Prayer

BURIAL: HOLY SILENCE

O death, where is your victory? O grave, where is your sting?
Thanks be to God who gives us victory through our Lord Jesus Christ.
Therefore, my beloved, be steadfast, immovable,
always abounding in the work of the Lord,
knowing that in the Lord your labor is not in vain.
The Apostle Paul (I Corinthians 15:55-58)

As anyone who has experienced the death of a family member or loved one can attest, death *hurts*. It hurts emotionally. It hurts spiritually. It hurts physically. When someone we love dies, a part of us also dies. Nor is it just the death of a person we love that results in a deep sense of loss. It can be the loss of a job, a relationship, our health, or a dream.

Grief is a funny process. The return to life is often slow, especially following a traumatic loss, which perhaps explains why Mary Magdalene did not initially recognize Jesus in the garden. Many times the process of grieving is just beginning when caring bystanders think it should be ending. Grief is not something we can put on a timeline. It ebbs and flows, catching us in unexpected moments. The fleeting smile of a stranger on the street, the first bloom of spring, the turn of a phrase—the simplest of things can bring back the pain and loss in the flash of a moment. Such is the nature of grief. It cannot be rushed or hurried. If we are to heal, grief must be honored.

The women understood this. They didn't run away from the pain of loss. As agonizing as it was to stand at the foot of the cross, it would have been more agonizing to wait at home for word of Jesus' death. Likewise, they honored the rhythms of Sabbath waiting until the dawn to go to the tomb with herbs and spices to embalm the body. The gift of ritual is important in times of loss. It allows us to grieve with intention.

Moreover, even with the beginning of healing, a remnant of sorrow remains. Just as wounds to the body scar the flesh, so grief can scar the soul. "Who has taken away my Lord?" Mary Magdalene asks. The one lost in death is not forgotten. The emptiness cannot be filled by new people or new activities. So powerful is death that it shapes our response to life from that point on. But, if we allow it, our experience of death can deepen and refine us ever more fully into the image of Christ.

As our faith attests, death does not have the last word. Resurrection, rising to new life, is also part of the grief process. Out of loss, new life does come! Just when we think we will never feel joy again, we find ourselves suffused with life. Just when the hollow of loneliness becomes unbearable, we come to actually enjoy the company of others. Our souls claim life as we encounter the love and compassion of God in the faces, words and care of those who surround us. God's victory over death comes to be understood in a new, more intimate way as we encounter the risen Lord in our midst.

Food for the Journey
- I Corinthians 15:55-58, O death, where is your victory?
- Matthew 27:45-56, Mark 15:33-41, Luke 23:44-49, The death of Jesus
- Matthew 27:57-61, Mark 15:42-47, Luke 23:50-56, John 19:38-42, The burial

Journey Questions
- How does Jesus' death and burial inform your understanding of death?
- Are there un-grieved losses in your life is God inviting you to grieve in this season?
- How is God calling you to enter into a place of holy silence between death and new life?

Journey Practice: Grieve Well
"Blessed are they who grieve[, ...] for they shall be comforted" (Matthew 5:4).

Elizabeth Kubler Ross, in her book *On Death and Dying*, identifies five distinct but interwoven stages to grief:
1. Denial (this *isn't happening* to me!)
2. Anger (why is this happening to *me?*)
3. Bargaining (I promise I'll be a better person *if...*)
4. Depression (I *don't care* anymore)
5. Acceptance (*I'm ready* for whatever comes)

This week, consider using the five stages of grief as a form of contemplative prayer. Ask yourself if there is any loss in your life that you are in denial about. Is there anger that you are stuffing down and ignoring? Often, our denial of anger evidences itself in other forms: weight gain (or loss), overwork, strained relationships. Are you holding yourself back from "letting go" by trying to hold on through bargaining? What signs of depression might others be noting? Dare to live these questions as they are often the precursor to acceptance, which is the foundation for living forward into God's future. Blessed are those who grieve, for they shall indeed be comforted!

Prayer for the Journey
Let us live in such a way
That when we die
Our love will survive
And continue to grow. Amen.
Michael Leunig, <u>A Common Prayer</u>

THREATENED WITH RESURRECTION

I am no longer afraid of death; I know well its dark and cold corridors leading to life. I am afraid rather of that life which does not come out of death which cramps our hands and retards our march. I am afraid of my fear and even more of the fear of others, who do not know where they are going, who continue clinging to what they consider to be life which we know to be death.

Julia Esquivel, <u>Threatened with Resurrection</u>

What does it mean to live as resurrection people? Mary wanted to hold onto Jesus once she recognized his voice. She wanted to reclaim the past. But Jesus is clear: we must live resurrection lives! We must give testimony to the power of resurrection even in the face of death, so Mary testifies! While the disciples do not initially believe her, tradition names her the apostle to the apostles—not a bad way to be remembered!

We live in a world where death dominates; where death is used as a means of power and control. I speak here not just of physical death, but also of spiritual death: a slow, painful eroding of the soul. The resurrection tells us that death no longer has the final word, that Jesus on the cross claimed victory over death once and for all. Yet we continue to allow our lives to be shaped and directed by death, rather than life. Perhaps this is because so much of life is lived in the face of death, deep down we do not really believe that God is victorious over the grave.

Julia Esquivel, elementary school teacher become activist, poet and minister, understands well the threat of death. As a native of Guatemala, she endured nearly thirty years of catastrophic political violence under the rule of a series of dictators. Esquivel watched as thousands of Maya, Quichez and other indigenous groups were savagely murdered. Against this bloody backdrop, Esquivel stood as a witness to God's justice and compassion, and acted as a healer amidst a land of suffering until she was forced into exile.

Esquivel knows the cost of resurrection living. Yet she also knows that death leads to life. She knows that a life not shaped by the paradox of crucifixion preceding resurrection is in truth, a living death. Both her life and her poetry are a testimony to resurrection living, for she lives the words she writes and writes the words she lives. May we, too, dare to live as resurrection people who are "no longer afraid of death, (but) rather of that life which does not come out of death."

Food for the Journey: The Resurrection
- Matthew 28:1-8
- Mark 16:1-8
- Luke 24:1-10
- John 20:1-8

Journey Questions
1. How does your experience of death shape your response to resurrection?
2. What does it mean to be "threatened with resurrection?"
3. What does it mean to live as resurrection people?

Journey Practice: Renewal of Baptismal Vows
It is not only appropriate, but even needful, for us to remember the promises made in baptism. They include renunciation and affirmation:

- Do you renounce evil, and its powers in the world, which defies God's righteousness and love? *I renounce them.*
- Do you renounce the ways of sin that separate you from the love of God? *I renounce them.*
- Do you turn to Jesus Christ and accept him as your Lord and Savior? *I do.*
- Do you intend to be Christ's faithful disciple, obeying his word, and showing his love, to your life's end? *I do.*

Prayer for the Journey
God of all life and goodness, we praise you for claiming us through our baptism and for upholding us by your grace. We remember your promises given to us in our baptism. Strengthen us by your Spirit, that we may obey your will and serve you with joy; through Jesus Christ our Lord. Amen.

The Journey:
Growing Up in Christ

Resurrection Blessings

Engagement
Call

The Sacramental Life
Community

Love
& Testing
Character

Grace-saturated Embrace
Core Identity in Christ

RESURRECTION BLESSINGS

"I have seen the Lord!"
Mary Magdalene (Matthew 20:18)

The One who was dead now lives. It is not just an empty tomb that attests to Jesus' rising, but also his post-resurrection appearances. He appears to Mary and the women in the garden, to the disciples in the Upper Room, later to Thomas behind locked doors; to Peter and the others on the beach; to the two disciples on the road to Emmaus; to the eleven before his Ascension; and then on the road to Damascus to the Apostle Paul. These resurrection sightings reflect the reality that the formational journey is but preparation for resurrection living.

Fully human, fully divine, Jesus models the way of transformation in and through his earthly journey. With the grace-saturated embrace, we discover what it means to be created in the image of God, fearfully and wonderfully made, heirs of God's salvation. With love and testing, we plumb the depths of our humanity. With engagement, we come to know what it is to have our hearts turned out to the world. With the sacramental life, we become intimate with the full depravity of humanity, a brokenness that lies not just without but also within.

With Pentecost comes the gift of the Spirit and the responsibility to live as resurrection people. The formational journey calls us to be attentive to each stage of the journey. Unless we have experienced the grace-saturated embrace, we cannot endure the love and testing that follows. Without engagement, we are not readied to live the sacramental life. But, when we engage the journey in all its fullness, we are blessed to live as resurrection people.

Meister Eckhart believed that "each human soul is a footprint of God." As we become like Jesus and make the journey our home, our footprints bear God's love into the world—for we by love and for love were made. For those who dare to make the journey our home, the amazing gift is that we come to embody Christ as he is formed in us. Such embodiment results in creativity, generativity, and meaningful service in the name of Jesus.

Resurrection blessings as you make the journey your home!

THE FAITH OF DOUBTING THOMAS

Doubting Thomas. That's how most of us remember him: the disciple who doubted the testimony of the others. The disciple who would not believe that Jesus had risen from the dead until he had seen him with his own eyes and touched his wounds with his own hands.

It is not hard to understand why Thomas questioned the news of Jesus' resurrection. He had lost the most important person in his life in a brutal and traumatic manner. He was there when Jesus was arrested in the dark of night. He had heard the cries of "Crucify! Crucify him!" He knew without a doubt that Jesus had died on the cross.

Nothing in his life could have prepared him for resurrection. His grief and pain were too raw. While his faith called him to believe a reality he had not yet experienced, the death was too real to discount. But then Jesus appeared to him as he had to the others. There in the Upper Room, he said to Thomas: "Put your fingers here and see my hands; put out your hand and place it in my side." In that moment, Jesus lovingly and gently invited Thomas to live not in the shadow of death, but the light of resurrection. He let him know he was alive. Thomas' response reflects his joy and his faith: "My Lord and my God!"

Thomas was a man for whom faith was never easy. He was a man of questions and doubts. If we're honest, his questions mirror our questions—questions that we are sometimes afraid to ask. Question like, "Lord, we don't know where you are going, so how can we know the way?" (John 14:5), a question that gifts us with Jesus' testimony that he is "the way, the truth, and the life" (14:6).

Like Thomas, we too struggle to understand what it means to live as resurrection people in the face of death. It is important to remember that doubt is not the opposite of believing. Rather, it is a form of believing. As another disciple said, "I believe, help my unbelief" (Mark 9:24). It is reassuring to know that in the midst of believing, there is a place for doubts and questions.

As we come to bear Christ into the lives of others who doubt, may we remember the paradox of Thomas, who was willing to follow Jesus to his death, only to receive the invitation to follow him into resurrection living.

Food for the Journey
- John 14: 1-14, Thomas acknowledges that he doesn't know the way.
- John 20:24-31, Jesus appears to Thomas
- Hebrews 11:1-17, By faith

Journey Questions
1. How does Thomas' story inform your journey? How do you respond to Jesus' words to Thomas? What words might Jesus speak to you?
2. What doubts shape your faith?
3. What does it mean to believe even with unbelief?

Journey Practice: Experiencing God
"In the days ahead, you will either be a mystic (one who has experienced God for real) or nothing at all" (Karl Rainer, 20th century mystic).

Even as Jesus honored Thomas' need to see and touch, he told him, "Because you have seen me, you have believed; blessed are those who have not seen and yet have believed" (John 20:29). To live as resurrection people requires us to nurture the mystic within.

Simply put, a mystic is a person "who has experienced God for real." In what ways have you experienced God? How do those experiences confirm (or differ) from what you have been told about God? This next week, attend to the ways in which you encounter God in your daily living. Where do you find God most present? Are there areas of your life where you feel God's absence? What does it mean for you to "experience God for real"?

Journey Prayer
Below is an ancient Easter hymn attributed to Hippolytus of Rome from the early third century. This week, each evening before bed, take time to pray through these ancient words and ponder the mystery of resurrection:

The shadows seized a body and found it was God. They reached for earth and what they held was heaven. They took what they could see; it was what no one sees. Where is death's goad? Where is the shadow's victory? Christ is risen; the world below is in ruins. Christ is risen; the spirits of evil are fallen. Christ is risen; the angels of God are rejoicing. Christ is risen; the tombs are void of their dead. Christ has indeed arisen from the dead; the first of those who sleep.
Glory and power are his for ever and ever. Amen.

THE ROAD TO LIFE

It is the road all of us will walk at some point in our lives. The paradox is that the road to life often feels like the road to death at first. For that reason, most of us do not willingly choose to walk this road for we know that it will involve pain and even loss.

It is the road you walk when you've been laid off and don't know where to turn next. It is the road you walk when your marriage falls apart. It is the road you walk when the one you loved more than life itself dies. It is the road you walk when your children make decisions you can't fix. It is the road that is marked by disappointment and sadness. But it is also the road that can lead to abundant life.

This is the same road that the two unnamed disciples walked back to Emmaus on the first Easter eve. A seven mile walk home. Home, to the empty house left behind. Home, to piled up mail. Home, to a life that will never be the same.

As they walked, they talked about the roller-coaster events of the last three days: the trial, the death, and the tomb, the news of the empty tomb and the women's testimony that he was alive! What were they to make of that?

Death they knew. But resurrection? This was their talk when the stranger joined them. Was he the only one who hadn't heard? They had so hoped (past tense). But death puts an end to hope.

It is then that stranger explodes, "Oh, how foolish, how slow of heart! Is your vision that stunted? Has the structure of the way things have been so blinded you that you can't see God's new born out of death?" Starting with Moses and working his way through the prophets, the Jesus then opens the scriptures to them. And they hang on his words as he reveals a God who shares in their suffering, a God who meets them in the place of their brokenness and offers them new life.

Our God still walks the road with us, inviting us to new life in him. The road to life requires but one thing and that is to name our broken places that we might offer them to God for healing, that we might choose life in him. What in you is broken and in need of healing? On what road do you walk as a congregation? Know that God walks with you and desires to meet you in the very midst of brokenness, for that is the place where God works best.

Food for the Journey
- Genesis 12:1-9, The Call of Abram
- Hebrews 11:17-30, By faith
- Luke 24:13-25, On the road to Emmaus

Journey Questions
1. Have you walked the road to Emmaus? When was that? What did it have to teach you about the sacramental life?
2. Where in your life have you encountered Jesus in the breaking of bread?
3. How is Jesus calling you to be broken that you might be shared?

Journey Practice: Walking with Jesus
Sometimes we find ourselves on the road following a dramatic event: the death of a loved one, the end of a dream, or an unexpected change in circumstances. Other times, the circumstances that place us on the road are more subtle, the result of gradual changes that we hadn't even noticed, the combination of a few minor alterations. Either way, we find ourselves on the road of loss.

Take some time to reflect on where you find yourself on your life's road. Is there brokenness that needs to be named and offered to Jesus? Are there joys in the midst of challenge for which you need to thank God? How is God seeking to offer himself to you in this time? Will you receive him and his invitation to life, even (or especially) if it calls you out of habits that have provided a sense of safety and identity for you?

Spend some time with God in prayer. Dare to offer your insights born of prayer with a trusted friend, making a commitment to live forward into God's call.

Journey Prayer
O unfamiliar God, we seek you in places you have already left,
and fail to see you even when you stand before us.
Grant us so to recognize your strangeness that we need not cling to our familiar grief,
but may be freed to proclaim resurrection in the name of Christ. Amen.
Janet Morley, <u>All Desires Known</u>

BREAKFAST ON THE BEACH

Feed my sheep. Tend my flock.
Jesus (John 21:15)

Even after the resurrection, the shame of the betrayal stayed with him. He had been called by Jesus to become a fisher of men and women. He had been called by Jesus to build his church. But all he felt capable of doing was to return to his nets and boat, to run from Jesus' call, a call that reminded him of his failure to support the man he loved and to stand by him in a time of trial.

For Peter, Jesus had special instructions. He was to "tend his flock [...] and feed his sheep." Three times Jesus asked Peter, "Do you love me?" Three times, Peter grieved by his past and pained by the question, answered, "Yes, Lord, you know that I love you." Three times, through word and deed, Jesus releases Peter from his shame and reminds him of his call: "Feed my sheep. Tend my flock."

Too often, we allow past mistakes and failures to get in the way of Jesus' love and his call. We fail to realize that God uses all things to shape and equip us to heed his call. Jesus reached into Peter's pain and brokenness on the beach that day. He fed him. He forgave him. He called him. Just as he feeds, forgives and calls us. Don't let anything in your past keep you from heeding God's call. Jesus through his death and resurrection has released you from bondage and sets you free to serve.

To be able to feed others requires integration of our whole selves. It calls for generativity born of forgiveness of self and others as we learn from our past mistakes and reclaim who we are in Christ. Only then can we fully relate to others in their need and failure.

Only then can we tend and feed.

Food for the Journey
- Psalm 23, The Good Shepherd
- Acts 2:14-40, Peter addresses the crowd
- John 21: 15-19, Breakfast on the beach

Journey Questions
1. Can you relate to Peter's denial? In what way?
2. What does Jesus' conversation with Peter have to teach us about forgiveness?
3. What aspect of your past is Jesus asking you to release to him in order to heed God's call?

Journey Practice: Pondering Incarnation
"The Word became flesh and blood and moved into the neighborhood" (John 1:14, *The Message*).

Incarnation remains a difficult lesson to learn. Even after the resurrection, Peter returned to his nets, bound by the shame of his denial. But Jesus came into our neighborhoods that we might have life. And he met Peter in his brokenness, forgiving him and charging him to "tend his flock and feed his sheep." Our call is to bear Jesus' incarnation into the world, meeting people in their brokenness, offering them not only healing, but also extending God's call to serve.

This week, take some time to prayerfully ponder the Prologue of John. Read through John 1:1-18 in several translations. Grapple with God's call to you in light of the reality that "the Word became flesh and blood, and moved into the neighborhood." Then spend some time pondering Gregory of Nyssa's challenge that sin happens whenever we refuse to keep growing. How is God calling you to grow? How are you to practice incarnation and embody Jesus?

Prayer for the Journey
Christ our friend,
You ask for our love,
In spite of our betrayal.
Give us courage to embrace forgiveness,
Know you again,
And trust in ourselves. Amen.
All Desires Known

ASCENSION BLESSINGS

When you're waiting, you're not doing nothing.
You're doing the most important something there is.
You're allowing your soul to grow up.
If you can't be still and wait,
you can't become what God created you to be.
Contemporary Monastic

I love Jesus' last words to his disciples before his Ascension. Roughly translated, he tells them to hurry up and wait—wait to be empowered by the Holy Spirit before charging forth to do ministry in his name (Acts 1:4-5). Jesus knew that without the power of the Holy Spirit there was no way that they could accomplish the mission to which he was sending them: to make disciples in Jerusalem, Judea, Samaria, and to the ends of the world (Acts 1:8). I sense he also knew that the disciples would not take the time to wait upon the Spirit, unless he was very clear about the reason for such waiting. Simply put, they were oblivious to their need for the empowerment of the Paraclete promised at the Last Supper.

Like, the disciples, we would do well to heed Jesus' instruction to wait before charging forth to launch a new ministry. Of course, it is important to remember that Biblical waiting is born of an expectancy that God is at work. Such waiting is not "dead time," but involves our whole being as we prepare for the advent of the Holy Spirit into our lives.

The disciples, upon returning to the Upper Room, joined together in prayer, study, and fellowship. So too, we must commit ourselves to prayer and study and fellowship if our hearts are to be readied for the in- dwelling of the Spirit. As one monastic put it: "When you're waiting, you're not doing nothing. You're doing the most important something there is. You're allowing your soul to grow up. If you can't be still and wait, you can't become what God created you to be."

Food for the Journey
- Psalm 46:10, Be still and know that I am God
- Matthew 28:16-20, The Great Commission
- Acts 1-2:1, Ascension instructions

Journey Questions

1. On a scale of one (low) to ten (high), how would you rate your ability to wait? Reflect on a recent experience of waiting—be it in line at a store, or for a friend or family member, or a package to arrive, or an event to occur. What was your attitude toward waiting? Was it anxious? Anticipatory? Impatient? Excited? Resistant? What do your emotions about waiting have to tell you?

2. Name a moment in the past week when you have been still. What did you experience in that moment? How does it inform your waiting upon God?

3. How is God, in this season, calling you to be still that you might become the person God created you to be?

Journey Practice: Waiting and Stillness

"People who wait have received a promise that allows them to wait. They have received something that is at work in them, like a seed that has started to grow. This is very important. We can only really wait if what we are waiting for has already begun for us. So waiting is never a movement from nothing to something. It is always a movement from something to something else" (Henri Nouwen, *A Spirituality of Waiting*).

There is a wonderful Taizé chant that calls us to wait upon the Lord. Taken directly from scripture, the chant is only two stanzas: "Wait for the Lord whose day is near. Wait for the Lord. Take heart. Don't fear."

Carmelite Reformer and mystic, Teresa of Avila advises us to "settle ourselves in stillness and we will come upon him in ourselves." Perhaps, she had been thinking of the Psalmist charge to "Be still and know that I am God" (46:10). Yet, in truth, how many still moments do we truly have in our lives? Our calendars reflect the craziness of our schedules. This week, take time apart with God, a daily moment of stillness simply to be and delight yourself in the Lord.

Prayer for the Journey

O God, you withdraw from our sight that you may be known by our love:
Help us to enter the cloud where you are hidden,
And surrender all our certainty to the darkness of faith.
In Jesus Christ, Amen.
All Desires Known

COME, CELEBRATE ME HOME

Please, celebrate me home, Give me a number,
Please, celebrate me home Play me one more song,
That I'll always remember, And I can recall,
Whenever I find myself too all alone, I can sing me home.
Kenny Loggins

Some will remember Kenny Loggins' Christmas song, "Please Celebrate Me Home." Haunting and filled with yearning, the song speaks of the hunger that is within us all to come home. As philosopher Pascal reflects: "There is a God-shaped vacuum in the heart of every person which cannot be filled by any created thing, but only by God, the Creator, made known through Jesus." As we become like Jesus, we come to know the yearning as a gift that nurtures our relationship with God in Christ.

So also, we come to understand that we share a call to bear Christ into a world that is dislocated and displaced by change. A recent Harvard Business Review publication begins with these observations:

"Virtually everything we have taken for granted for hundreds, if not thousands, of years is in the midst of profound transformation. Our planet's climate is changing, and we are experiencing extreme, unpredictable weather and temperature changes that affect indigenous plants, farming, animals, and sea life. There is a rise in the number and severity of natural disasters—hurricanes, floods, and droughts. New diseases are on the rise, and HIV and AIDS continue to decimate populations of entire countries and all the sub-Saharan Africa" (Boyatzis & McKee, *Resonant Leadership*).

I'll stop before I immobilize us by the immensity of what we are experiencing. But I share these words to set in context God's call to us in this season.

There is a tendency in times of deep change to want to "go back" to simpler times. Deep down, we know that there is no going back. We know we can never change things by fighting an existing reality. To change something, we must build the new and then the old will fall away. As Isaiah clearly tells us, God is "about to do a new thing; now it springs forth, do you not perceive it? I (God) will make a way in the wilderness and rivers in the desert [...] for the people whom I formed for myself so that they might declare my praise" (Isaiah 43:19-21).

Marjorie Zoet Bankson defines call as "an invitation to wholeness, a spiritual prompting to complete the work of love that we are here to do." She invites us to explore God's call to build the new through a cycle that includes:

- Resistance: What are the patterns of resistance in your life right now? What do these patterns have to tell you about call?

- Reclaiming: In reclaiming, we seek the form behind our skills - the original seed of call, the DNA of our souls. Reclaiming is not simply a process of reminiscence but of observation and action. What essential part of you is God calling you to reclaim?

- Revelation: happens in the cusp between *kairos* and *chronos* time; it brings with it ambivalence and uncertainty, possibility and potential danger. This is the way of new vision being born. What has God revealed to your heart?

- Crossing Over: True revelation demands a response. It demands a "crossing over," coupled with a willingness to be changed, healed, and expanded as we confront the barriers between belief and embodiment. To cross over we must confront our fears. To what must you attend in order to cross over?

- Risk: Deep within us is planted the seed of new creation - dreams for a better world and wild hope that our visions can be realized. We need to act to make our dreams real. Risk is the courage to change. Risk requires that we be willing to fail as well as succeed, to be wrong as well as to be right. What is God calling you to risk?

- Relate: Call cannot be fully manifested without community. Community that takes seriously God's call understands the importance of shared purpose. Yet developing such community is neither easy nor orderly. To whom do you relate?

- Release: Completing the cycle of soul work means integration, endings, and release. Release calls for generativity as we give call away and begin the cycle anew. Release is a stage of rest and listening. Learning when to let go and when to hang on is the essence of release. What aspect of your present call is God asking you to release in order to live forward?

Even as the cry of our hearts is to "please, celebrate me home," we know that we are called to be Christ for the world and make the journey our home. The early church father Augustine assures us: "Ask not where our home is, because in the end we all come home to God."

Blessings as you make the journey your home!

Food for the Journey
- Isaiah 43: 14-21, A new thing
- Hebrews 12:1-3, Surrounded by such a great cloud of witnesses
- Luke 24:36-53, Jesus appears to the disciples

Journey Questions
1. What does the word "home" mean to you? How is God calling you to make the journey your home?
2. Marjorie Zoet Bankson defines "call as an invitation to wholeness, a spiritual prompting to complete the work of love that we are here to do." In what areas of your life is God inviting you to experience wholeness? Where do you experience spiritual promptings? How do they inform your sense of God?
3. What does it mean for "the old" to pass away? How is God seeking to do a "new thing" in you?

Journey Practice: Stewardship of Self
"Therefore, I urge you, brothers and sisters, in view of God's mercy, to offer your bodies as a living sacrifice, holy and pleasing to God—this is true worship" (Romans 12:1).

Stewardship of self begins with recognizing that everything we have and are is a gift from God. God's intention is that we are to live our lives as "living sacrifices." Yet the powers of seduction would have us deny God's call. Rather than living out of the abundance of God, we come to live out of a sense of scarcity. Selfishness replaces sacrifice. Anxiousness replaces joy. The full use of our spiritual gifts is thwarted. No longer are we growing in maturity in Christ. Ultimately, the practice of stewardship reveals what is in our heart.

The heart of worship is to seek to know and love God with the whole of our lives. The apostle Paul reminds us that true worship is the offering of our very selves. Come before God with an open heart and listening ear. Ponder the question: What do I value most? Then answer the question from the perspective of those closest to you and from the perspective of God. What do you learn about yourself through their eyes? What did you learn about yourself through God's eyes? In what ways does your life reflect "true worship" born of offering yourself as a "living sacrifice"? In what ways, do you find that you have failed to fully worship God? How might what you worship need to change?

Prayer for the Journey

Life is a journey with others;
We travel as a people, on a winding road.
We share our lives, our experiences, our hopes, our fears.
With joy and hope, we welcome other travelers to share our lives.
We learn from each other.
We laugh and cry with each other.
We are at home with each other.
Life is a series of hellos and goodbyes.
There are those who arrive to be with us
There are those who move ahead of us beyond death.
Both in the laying-hold and letting-go we celebrate God's goodness.
We affirm the Spirit's presence in the journey, in being home.

Blessings and Birthings

POSTSCRIPT: BECOME LIKE JESUS

The gospel simply stated is: Become like Jesus.
Henri Nouwen

Become like Jesus—become *ourselves!* Become the men and women God has created and called us to be. Isn't that at the heart of growing up in Christ? Isn't that what transformation is all about?

The word for transform in Greek is *morphoo* and it refers to the inward and real formation of the essential nature of a person. Paul uses the word in a number of places in the Epistles, including Galatians where he writes: "I labor until Christ is *formed*—*morphoo*—in you" (4:19). "I labor," Paul exhorts, until your core identity, character, and call are formed in and through the power of the Holy Spirit in service to God in Christ. Paul, in likening our formation to the growth of an embryo, reflects the reality that we are pregnant with more possibility than most of us can imagine.

In Romans, Paul calls us to be "conformed to the image of the Son." The word, *summorphizo,* means to have the same form as another, to shape a thing into a durable likeness. Spiritual growth is a molding process. We are to be to Christ as an image is to its original.

But, as Bob Quinn notes in *Deep Change*, "The problem is that to grow, to take the journeys on which our growth is predicated, we must confront our own immaturity, selfishness, and lack of courage. In a sense, life is all about our forceful, often overpowering need to take journeys, yet our tendency is to grip the swings ever more tightly."

The choice is ours. God invites us to become like Jesus through the formational journey, but the Spirit will not enter us by force or without our consent. Will we say yes to God's invitation?

Food for the Journey
- Romans 12:1-3, Transformed by the renewing of your mind
- II Corinthians 3:17-18, Transformed into Christ's likeness
- Galatians 4:19, Until Christ is formed

Journey Questions
1. Based upon your journey through this study, take some time to reflect on what it means to be transformed into the Lord's likeness with ever-increasing glory.
2. Reflect on a time when you yourself or another person experienced such transformation. What new behaviors emerged? What did you experience and learn?
3. Develop a shared covenant with your family, a fellow disciple, or your congregation in which you commit to "growing up in Christ."

Journey Practice: Resume
Write a resume of your core identity, character, and call (not your competencies or expertise). What does this reveal about who you are becoming? Are you following in the way of Christ?

Prayer for the Journey
We are all meant to be Godbearers.
What good is it to me if this eternal birth of the divine Son
takes place unceasingly, but does not take place within myself?
And, what good is it to me if Mary is full of grace if I am not also full of grace?
What good is it to me for the Creator to give birth to his Son
if I do not also give birth to him in my time and my culture?
This, then, is the fullness of time: When the Son of Man is begotten in us.
Meister Eckhart, 1260-1328, German Dominican Mystic

The Journey:
Growing Up in Christ

Epilogue: The Journey is Our Home!

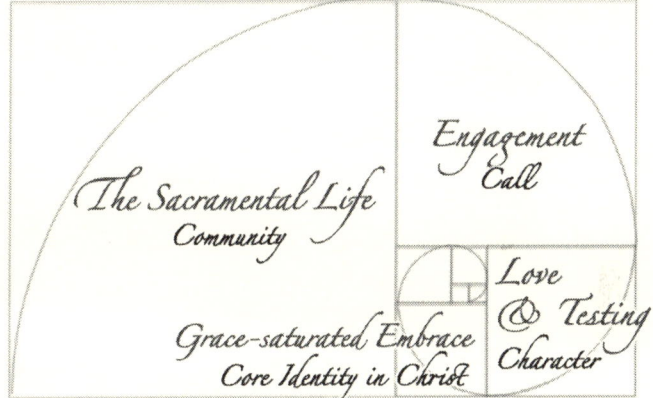

The Sacramental Life
Community

Engagement
Call

Grace-saturated Embrace
Core Identity in Christ

Love
& Testing
Character

EPILOGUE: THE JOURNEY IS OUR HOME

And what more shall I say?
Hebrews 11:32

Theological and Developmental Foundations

At first glance, these devotions seem rather simplistic, almost naïve. *The Journey: Growing Up in Christ* is not even a complete "telling" of Jesus earthly life; rather, it focuses on a formational set: from infancy, to adolescence, to young adulthood, to maturity. It looks at Jesus' earthly life as a model for how we are to live our lives as disciples. Simply put, *The Journey* is an invitation to become like Jesus.

The concept for the formational set comes from colleague and friend, Terry Wardle, with whom I taught at Ashland Theological Seminary for a number of years. Further insight comes from Paul Hiebert's *Transforming Worldviews: An Anthropological Understanding of How People Change* (Grand Rapids: Baker Academic, 2008). Both Terry and Paul speak to the impact of the "bounded" and "centered" sets upon the American church, often resulting in either an over-emphasis on law and order or an over-emphasis on grace, respectively. As a result, neither set provides an intentional means by which to be "transformed into the image of Christ" (II Corinthians 3:17-18).

Of particular challenge for Christians is moving beyond the "ought" self. Understanding of the "ought" self is drawn from Higgins' *Self-Discrepancy Theory* (1987) in which the "ought" self represents the set of attributes that a person (or others) believes he or she should possess—as in a call to moral duty—in contrast to the "real" self (actually possessed) and "ideal" self (ideally possessed). In faith-based contexts, especially, the "ought" self can lead to legalism and a judgmental orientation disconnected from practice.

Developmental psychologists have long agreed that there are key movements in human development tied to key life questions. *The Journey: Growing Up in Christ* seeks to provide linkage between these developmental movements, life questions, and our formation in Christ Jesus' invites his disciples to "learn of me" (Matthew 11:29). We come to find his actions match his words. The message and the messenger are one and the same: In Jesus' formation is our formation.

THE FORMATIONAL JOURNEY IN SUMMARY

Developmental Stage	Life Questions	Formational Set
Infancy	Who am I?	Core Identity in Christ nurtured through the *grace-saturated embrace.*
Adolescence	What are my strengths?	Character transformed through *love and testing.*
Young Adult	What is my work?	Call as lived through *engagement* in the world.
Adult	What is my legacy?	Community realized through *the sacramental life.*

WAYS TO ENGAGE WITH
THE JOURNEY: GROWING UP IN CHRIST

The question has been asked, "What is the best way to participate in *The Journey*?" It has been designed in such a way that it can be used individually, in a small group, or as a worshipping community. I am told that pastors and leaders have used them both for Bible Study and also as a worship series. Colleagues trained as Formational Prayer Counselors have also used these materials in conjunction with their ministry of healing.

As noted above, *The Journey* follows the four movements of Jesus' earthly life. Each entry includes a reflection, scripture, questions, practice, and prayer. Because the reflections follow the pattern of Jesus' earthly journey, *The Journey* mirrors the movement of the liturgical church year from Advent to Pentecost. Two possible ways of using the materials in tandem with the liturgical church year are:

- As an annual devotion to begin with *All Saints Sunday* (the first Sunday in November), with Journey Preparations, using one entry a week through the course of a year;
- As a Lenten devotion, beginning with *Transfiguration Sunday* (the Sunday before Ash Wednesday), with Journey Preparations, using one entry a day.

That being said, these are not materials to be rushed. Our formation in Christ takes time and patience. Our growing up in Christ is the journey of a lifetime. Should you use these materials as a Lenten devotion, I encourage you to consider it an introduction to then return to at a more leisurely pace. Further, there is power in engaging an aspect of Jesus' earthly journey "out of season." To do so challenges preconceptions and offers new insights. Do not let the time of year hold you back from your formation.

The Journey: Growing Up in Christ is intentionally provided in small doses. We are a people on information overload. We do not need more to digest. Rather, we need learn a new way that balances our doing with being. The inclusion of Journey Practices with each reflection is intentional; they are not to be skipped over. If you do nothing else, engage the practice.

We are a people of habits. Neurological studies reveal that all habits are driven by cravings. The challenge, of course, is that not all habits are of God. The Old Testament warns us to "be careful that you do not forget the Lord your God" (Deuteronomy 8:11). The intent of the Journey Practices is to help us develop holy habits that shape and form our lives in response to the invitation of Jesus to follow him.

Acknowledgement must also be given to the many influences and sources referenced throughout the book. I am particularly indebted to the work of Dallas Willard and Ruth Haley Barton, along with many other fellow pilgrims. A selected bibliography is included for those who wish to read further. In addition, I've included the sources for the Journey Prayers. While there is a place for spontaneous prayer, so also it is good the pray with "the cloud of witnesses" (Hebrews 12:1). Through the years, I have been deeply touched by the gift of prayer that has come from both ancient and contemporary saints. In particular, you will find many entries from Michael Leunig, Janet Morley, Ted Loder, as well as prayers from the ancients. May they bless you as they have blessed me!

One final word: *The Journey: Growing Up in Christ* is an open conversation. I would love to hear from you about your journey. In what way have these materials been helpful to you in your faith journey? Are there materials you would like to share? If so, please email me at Deborah@MVPJourney.org. I look forward to hearing from you!

Truly, the journey is our home!

With love in Christ,
Deborah Anne Rundlett
Advent 2013

The Journey:
Growing Up in Christ

Journey Resources - Appendices

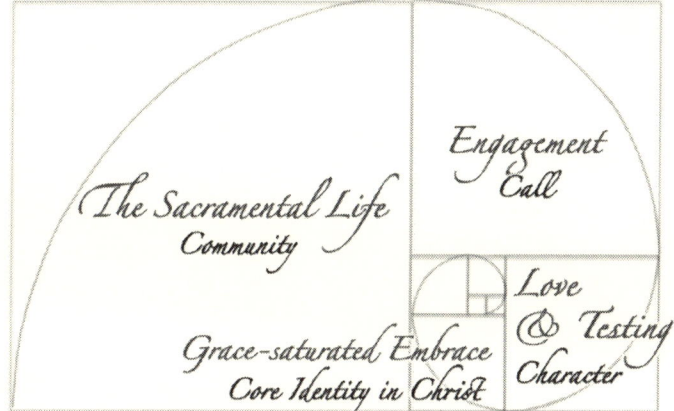

APPENDIX I:

The Journey
Weekly Focus and Journey Practices

AN INVITATION

Week	Focus	Journey Practice
1	**Two Metaphors** *Matthew 1-2* *Luke 1-2*	Know Your Story *Inhabit my heart (Ignatius)*
2	**Destination** *Galatians 4:19*	Pondering *God, help us to change (Leunig)*
3	**Itinerary** *Formational Journey*	Itinerary *Take, O take me as I am (Iona)*
4	**Terrain** *Psalm 139*	Rhythm *Dear God, we pray for another way*
5	**Compass** *Hebrews 2:2*	Calibration *Where I wander—You! (Levi)*
6	**Packing Instructions**	Packing *Pilgrim's Mass*

THE GRACE-SATURATED EMBRACE

Week	Focus	Journey Practice
7	**Annunciation** *Luke 1:26-38*	Interspersed Prayer *God be with the mother...*
8	**Dreams** *Joel 2:28-32* *Acts 10:9-23* *Matthew 1:18-25*	Journal Your Dreams *We give thanks for the darkness of the night...*
9	**Birth in the Spirit** *Ezekiel 37:1-14* *Acts 19:1-17* *I Corinthians 6: 19-20* *Matthew 1:18-25*	Remember Your Baptism *Deliver me, O God, BCP*
10	**Community** *Ruth 1:16-22* *Acts 2:42-47* *Luke 1:39-66*	The One Anothers *God of community (All Desires Known)*
11	**Celebration** *Exodus 15* *I Thessalonians 5:12-28* *Luke 2:8-20*	Celebration *Isaac of Stella blessing*
12	**Consecration** *I Samuel 1:21-28* *Acts 9:1-19* *Luke 2:21-40*	Anointing *Take, Lord, and receive all my liberty (Ignatius)*
13	**Protection** *Exodus 2:1-10* *Galatians 5:1-21* *Matthew 2:13-18*	Margins *Lord, I am willing to receive (Calhoun)*
14	**Growth in the Secret Place** *Exodus 2:11-22* *Galatians1:11-24* *Matthew 2:13-18*	Finding Your Secret Place *Circle me, Lord (David Adams)*
15	**Return to Nazareth** *Exodus 2:1-10* *Romans 12:3-8* *Luke 2:39-40*	Roots *Blessed be the people we carry in our blood (Jan Richardson)*
16	**In the Temple** *Proverbs 8:32-36* *Ephesians 3:14-21* *Luke 2:41-52*	At the feet of Jesus *Ephesians 3:14-21*

LOVE AND TESTING

Week	Focus	Journey Practice
17	**Dust and Delight** *Genesis 2:4-7* *I Corinthians 15:35-58* *Matthew 11:28-30*	Resting in Jesus *The Message, Matthew 11:28-30*
18	**The Potter's Hand** *Jeremiah 18:1-6, Psalm 139* *II Corinthians 4:7-9*	Making Pottery *Spirit of the Living God, Fall Afresh*
19	**Behold the Lamb of God!** *Isaiah 40:1-5, Acts 2:14-41* *Luke 3:1-22*	Confession of Faith with Psalm 51 *God help us to find our confession (Leunig)*
20	**Entering the Mess** *Jeremiah 29:1-11* *Romans 8:31-39* *Matthew 3:13-17*	Entering the Mess *Come, O Holy Spirit, come as Holy Fire (BCW)*
21	**The Wilderness Journey** *Deuteronomy 8:15-16* *Galatians 5:13-26* *Mark 1:9-13*	In the Wilderness *Spirit of Integrity (All Desires Known)*
22	**Crucibles** *Zechariah 13:1-9* *Acts 5:25-42* *Matthew 2:1-17*	Crucible Letter *Purify My Heart (Doerksen)*
23	**Shadow Boxing** *Genesis 1* *Romans 12:1-3* *Luke 4:1-13*	Shadow Boxing *O Eternal One (Guerrillas of Grace)*
24	**Sin Happens!** *Psalm 51* *Romans 7:7-25* *Luke 11:24-26*	Pondering Sin *Take, O Lord, all my liberty (Ignatius)*
25	**God Power and *Kenosis*** *Micah 6:6-8* *Philippians 2:1-11* *John 3:22-36*	Emptied! *Empty Me (Guerrillas of Grace)*
26	**And the Angels Ministered** *Genesis 28:10-22* *I Peter 3:8-9, Matthew 4:11*	Stress and Renewal *We Give You Thanks (More than Words)*

ENGAGEMENT

Week	Focus	Journey Practice
27	**A Message to Proclaim** *Isaiah 61, Acts 2:14-41* *Luke 4:14-30*	Radical Hospitality *Fearful God (All Desires Known)*
28	**The Calling of the Twelve** *Exodus 18:13-27* *Romans 12:1-8* *Mark 3:13-15*	Heeding God's Call *Look at your hands, see and touch (A Wee Worship Book)*
29	**Teaching in Parables** *Isaiah 11:1-9* *I Corinthians 15:50-58* *Matthew 13:35-35*	Becoming a Parabolic Event *Clement of Rome*
30	**Healing** *Psalm 30, James 5:14-16* *John 5*	Attend a Healing Service *O God, gather me to be with you (Guerrillas of Grace)*
31	**Feeding** *Zechariah 7:8-10* *Galatians 4:8-20, John 6*	Communion *O God, you have so greatly loved us*
32	**Before Dawn: Time with the Father** *Psalm 42, Romans 8:18-39* *Mark 1:35-39*	Silence & Solitude *Richard Rolle*
33	**Who Do You Say That I Am?** *Deuteronomy 6:4-9* *I Corinthians 1:17-25* *Matthew 16:13-20*	Give Testimony *God be with those who explore the cause of understanding (Leunig)*
34	**Transfigured!** *Hebrews 12:1-13* *Matthew 17:1-13*	The Heart of Worship *Collect, BCP*
35	**Woe to You!, Scribes and Pharisees!** **Jersualem, Jerusalem!** *Joshua 1, Romans 5:1-5* *Matthew 23:23-26*	Seven Habits *Richard Foster* Weep, Worship and Walk *Psalm 122*

LIVING THE SACRAMENTAL LIFE

Week	Focus	Journey Practice
36	**From Hosanna to Crucify!** *Isaiah 58:1-12, Philippians 2:12-18, Mark 14-16*	Were You There? *Empty me, Lord*
37	**Upper Room Instructions** *Jeremiah 31:30-34 I Corinthians 13, John 14:34*	The One Anothers (encore!) *Help us accept each other*
38	**Is it I, Lord?** *Psalm 124, Matthew 26:17-30 I Corinthians 15:1-11*	Pondering Betrayal *Christ our victim*
39	**Gethsemane: Watch with Me** *Matthew 26:36-48 Mark 14:32-41 Luke 22:39-46*	Relinquishment *A Prayer of Relinquishment*
40	**Denial** *Matthew 26:31-35; Mark 14:27-31; Luke 22:31-35, Mark 14:66-72, Luke 22:54-62, John 18:15-27,*	F.A.C.E. (David Richo) *How then shall we live?*
41	**What is Truth?** *Ephesians 4:1-6, Galatians 4:8-20, John 14:1-14; 18:28-40*	Truth-telling *In order to be truthful*
42	**The Cross** *Malachi 3:1-3, Matthew 16:21-28, Luke 23:26-49*	Crucifixion *That which is Christ-like…*
43	**Golgotha: It is Finished!** *Matthew 27:32-44, Mark 15:22-32, Luke 23:33-43 John 19:17-24*	Prayer at the Cross *God help us*
44	**Burial: Holy Silence** *I Corinthians 15:55-58 Matthew, Mark, Luke—Death & Burial accounts*	Grieve Well *Let us live in such a way*
45	**Threatened with Resurrection** *Matthew, Mark, Luke, John—Resurrection accounts*	Renewal of Baptismal Vows *God of all life and goodness*

RESURRECTION BLESSINGS

Week	Focus	Journey Practice
46	**The Faith of Doubting Thomas** *John 14:1-4* *John 20:24-31* *Hebrews 11:1-17*	Experiencing God *Easter Prayer, Hippolytus*
47	**The Road to Life** *Genesis 12:1-9* *Hebrews 11:17-30* *Luke 24:13-25*	Walking with Jesus *O unfamiliar God*
48	**Breakfast on the Beach** *Psalm 23* *Acts 2:14-40* *John 21:15-19*	Pondering Incarnation *Christ our Friend*
49	**Ascension Blessings** *Psalm 46:10* *Matthew 28:16-20* *Acts 1:1-2:1*	Waiting and Stillness *O God, you withdraw from our sight*
50	**Come, Celebrate Me Home** *Isaiah 43:14-21* *Hebrews 12:1-3* *Luke 24:36-53*	Stewardship of Self *Life is a journey with others…*
51	**Postscript:** *Become like Jesus* *Romans 12:1-3* *II Corinthians 3:17-18* *Galatians 4:19*	Resume *We are all meant to be Godbearers*

APPENDIX II:
THE JOURNEY NAUTILUS ILLUSTRATION

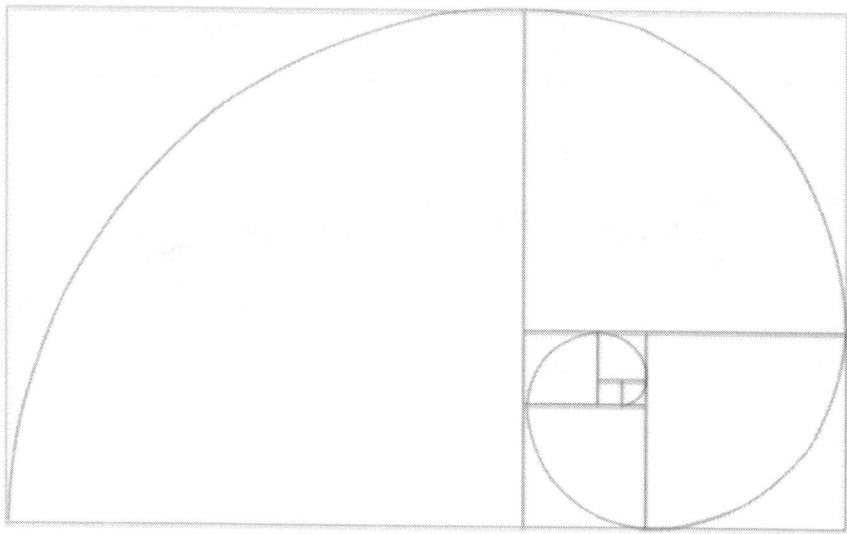

APPENDIX III:
THE "ONE ANOTHERS"

Printable cards of the "One Anothers" referenced in "The Grace-Saturated Embrace" can be found at www.mvpjourney.org and clicking on the link to resources for *The Journey: Growing Up in Christ.*

APPENDIX IV:
SELECTED BIBLIOGRAPHY

Arnold, D.W.H. (1991). *Prayers of the Martyrs*. Grand Rapids, MI: Zondervan Publishing.

Barton, R.H. (2006). *Sacred Rhythms: Arranging Our Lives for Spiritual Transformation*. Downers Grove, IL: InterVarsity Press.

Bass, D. (ed.) (1997). *Practicing Our Faith: A Way of Life for Searching People*. San Francisco, CA: Jossey-Bass, Inc.

Broyles, A. (et al). (2002). *Soul Tending: Life-Forming Practices for Older Youth and Young Adults*. Nashville, TN: Abingdon Press.

Calhoun, A. A. (2005). *Spiritual Disciplines Handbook: Practices that Transform Us*. Downers Grove, IL: InterVarsity Press.

Church, F. F. & Mulry, T.J. (1988). *The Macmillan Book of Early Christian Prayers*. New York, NY: Collier Macmillan Canada, Inc.

Dean, K.C. & Foster, R. (1998). *The Godbearing Life: The Art of Soul Tending for Youth Ministry*. Nashville, TN: Upper Room Books, Inc.

deSilva, D.A. (2008). *Sacramental Life: Spiritual Formation Through the Book of Common Prayer*. Downers Grove, IL: InterVarsity Press.

Ford, M. (2006). *Traditions of the Ancients: Vintage Faith Practices for the 21st Century*. Nashville, TN: Broadman and Holman Publishers.

Foster, R. (1998). *Celebration of Discipline: The Path to Spiritual Growth (25th Anniversary Edition)*. New York, NY: HarperCollins Publishing.

Jones, T. (2003). *Soul Shaper: Exploring Spirituality and Contemplative Practices in Youth Ministry*. Grand Rapids, MI: Zondervan Publishing.

Leunig, M. (1990). *A Common Prayer*. North Blackburn, Victoria: Collins Dove.

---. (1991). *The Prayer Tree*. North Blackburn, Victoria: Dove Publications.

Loder, T. (1984). *Guerrillas of Grace*. San Diego, CA: LuraMedia.

McDonald, G. (2004). *The Disciple Making Church: From Dry Bones to Spiritual Vitality.* Grand Haven, MI: FaithWalk Publishing.

Mitchell, R.C. & Riccuiti, G.A. (1991). *Birthings and Blessings: Liberating Worship Services for the Inclusive Church.* New York, NY: The Crossroad Publishing Company.

Morely, J. (1992). *All Desires Known: Inclusive Prayers for Worship and Meditation (Expanded Edition).* Harrisburg, PA: Morehouse Publishing.

---, (ed.) (1992). *Bread of Tomorrow: Prayers for the Church Year.* Maryknoll, NY: Orbis Books.

Presbyterian Church (U.S.A.) Prepared by the Theology and Worship Ministry Unit for the PC(USA) and the Cumberland Presbyterian Church. (1993). *Book of Common Worship.* Louisville, KY: Westminster/John Knox Press.

Scazzero, P. (2006). *Emotionally Healthy Spirituality: Unleash a Revolution in Your Life in Christ.* Nashvile, TN: Thomas Nelson.

Smith, J.B. (2010). *The Good and Beautiful Community: Following the Spirit, Extending Grace, Demonstrating Love.* Downers Grove, IL: InterVarsity Press.

---. (2009). *The Good and Beautiful God: Falling in Love with the God Jesus Knows.* Downers Grove, IL: InterVarsity Press.

---. (2009). *The Good and Beautiful Life: Putting on the Character of Christ.* Downers Grove, IL: InterVarsity Press.

Thompson, M. (1995). *Soul Feast: An Invitation to the Christian Spiritual Life.* Louisville, KY: Westminster/John Knox Press.

Wardle, T. (2004). *Draw Close to the Fire: Finding God in the Darkness.* Abilene, TX: Leafwood Publishers.

---. (2007). *Strong Winds and Crashing Waves: Meeting Jesus in the Memories of Traumatic Events.* Abilene, TX: Leafwood Publishers.

Wild Goose Worship Group. (1999). *A Wee Worship Book: Fourth Incarnation.* Chicago, IL: GA Publications, Inc.

Willard, D. (2002). *Renovation of the Heart: Putting on the Character of Christ.* Colorado Springs, CO: NavPress.

---. (1998). *The Spirit of the Disciplines: Understanding How God Changes Lives.* New York, NY: HarperCollins.

Wright, W.M. (2003). *Seasons of a Family's Life: Cultivating the Contemplative Spirit at Home.* San Francisco, CA: Jossey-Bass, a Wiley Imprint.

Yaconelli, M. (2006). *Contemplative Youth Ministry: Practicing the Presence of Jesus.* Grand Rapids, MI: Zondervan Publishing.

ABOUT THE AUTHOR

Debbie is a disciple of Jesus who loves God and loves people.
The Journey: Growing Up in Christ is born out of her work as a pastor,
professor and coach. Her passions include cooking for friends and family,
Taekwondo, and travel. Truly, the journey is her home!

Made in the USA
Charleston, SC
14 March 2014